H. C. FOR LIFE,
THAT IS TO SAY . . .

MERIDIAN

Crossing Aesthetics

Werner Hamacher

Editor

Translated, with additional notes,
by Laurent Milesi and
Stefan Herbrechter

Stanford
University
Press

———

Stanford
California
2006

H. C. FOR LIFE,
THAT IS TO SAY . . .

Jacques Derrida

Stanford University Press
Stanford, California

H.C. for Life, That Is to Say . . . was originally published in French in 2000
under the title *H.C. pour la vie, c'est à dire . . .* © 2000, Éditions Galilée.

This book has been published with the assistance of the
French Ministry of Culture—National Center for the Book.

Library of Congress Cataloging-in-Publication Data

Derrida, Jacques.
 [H. C. pour la vie, c'est à dire—English]
 H. C. for life, that is to say— / Jacques Derrida ; translated by Laurent
Milesi and Stephen Herbrechter.
  p. cm.—(Meridian, crossing aesthetics)
 Includes bibliographical references.
 ISBN-13: 978-0-8047-5401-9 (cloth : alk. paper)
 ISBN-13: 978-0-8047-5402-6 (pbk. : alk. paper)
  1. Cixous, Hélène, 1937– I. Title. II. Series: Meridian (Stanford, Calif.)

PQ2663.19Z62813 2003
848'.91409—DC22

2006009690

Typeset by Tim Roberts in 10.9/13 Garamond
and Lithos display

Contents

Translator's Preface:
Taking Sides in Translation

As the text itself records on a couple of occasions, *H.C. pour la vie, c'est à dire . . .* was first given as the inaugural lecture of the Cixous conference held at Cerisy-la-Salle in June 1998; it was subsequently published as part of the proceedings volume entitled *Hélène Cixous: Croisées d'une oeuvre* (ed. Mireille Calle-Gruber [Paris: Galilée, 2000], pp. 13–140).[1] This "official" homage, one of several textual crossings between Cixous and Derrida during the last decade, marked a special moment in some thirty-five years of a close intellectual as well as personal friendship, which *H.C. pour la vie* and subsequently Cixous's fictional-critical *Portrait de Jacques Derrida en Jeune Saint Juif* recall at great length, from their first "real" meeting at a Paris café in 1963, some seven years after the primal scene of a "missed encounter" (her seeing him from behind, lecturing on death)—which one could choose to read as a contemporary restaging of the famous postcard featuring Plato dictating behind Socrates' back.

Perhaps on account of this privileged bond between two "men of letters" particularly adept at pushing the most resistingly idiomatic elements of the French language to (or even beyond) their limits,[2] *H.C. pour la vie* demands a most vigilant reading at every instant, even (or especially) at the most deceptively inconspicuous turns of Derrida's writing. More than is usually the case in Derrida's celebratory lectures, *H.C. pour la vie* imports Cixous's own inventive genius. The resulting *encomium to Hélène* thus oscillates, beyond Derrida's own recognizable modes, between the tribute of *citation* (or—since he often resorts to English, "one of all her tongues"—*quotation*) and translation. Derrida not only signs and countersigns Cixous's writing with a customary gift of what he here calls "grace" or "salutation," but more specifically he "(re)initializes" inexorably, that is to say, "pre-names" [French *prénom*: forename, first name] constantly, by deploying her initials, H.C. (the latter, he reminds us, almost sounding like *c'est*), and begins again all the time, adding his own palinodic, (auto-)citational *Recommencements* to Cixous's works, one of whose titles was *Les Commencements*. Linguistically (in passages shot through with deliberate anglicisms) and stylistically, *H.C. pour la vie* is thus already a cross and "in translation," possibly even written "against translation"—though, unlike several other texts, Derrida never explicitly challenges his future translators—or else already "on the side of translation," signaling in its direction (*du côté de la traduction*). The necessary and impossible task of the translator is nowhere more acute than when the very grammar of the modular verb *pouvoir* is being reconfigured, by enlisting the help of the verbal as well as the nominal range of the English *might*. Faced with such a linguistic "aporia" touching on the core of what an "idiom" is—an aporia through which much of the philosophical argument of *H.C. pour la vie* is conducted—we have likewise resorted to bending the target language to the same strictures of "experilous" experimentation to which the "original" language has been subjected, glossing the most problematic cruxes in concise endnotes. In other words, echoing one of the structural chains running through the work, we had to take sides and stand resolutely on the side (*côté*) or even shore (*côte*) of a transgeneric trans-lation, from Derrida to Cixous and back (and across into English), from English within French into English, sometimes quoting or adapting existing translations, in order to bring across to the reader a comparable experience of the subtle uniqueness of *H.C. pour la vie* in the Derridean corpus. During this relentless task, Valerie Minogue, emeritus professor of French at the University of Wales Swansea, has been unsparing of her generous efforts and literary sensitivity in both languages, and we are immensely indebted to her for her unerring advice and suggestions. We also wish to thank Catherine Belsey and Beverley Bie Brahic for their judicious comments, the whole editorial team at Stanford University Press, in particular Elizabeth Berg, for their support and professional care, and Hélène Cixous herself for her warm encouragement throughout.

Finally, one cannot silence another thematic opposition of sides at work throughout Derrida's text, one that was to take on a bitterly ironic note of foresight—more so than the "almost somnambulistic . . . fore-sight" he retrospectively associates with his initial perception of Cixous's early prose—which no work of translation or translation as working through could hope to transcend. On October 8, 2004, while this impossible rendering was still in progress, it became no longer possible to read and translate the near-final words of *H.C pour la vie,* "Death would be on my side and life on hers," as if they were a mere metaphor clinching a crucial thread of the book to a satisfactory close: Jacques Derrida died—prematurely (but can it be otherwise?)—from side effects of pancreatic cancer. And the grief that we as translators felt, like the rest of the vast community of friends and followers to whom he had given so much "without counting," made it poignantly more difficult to complete the translation of a work whose near-constant reminders of the obsessive preponderance of death in Derrida's thought stalk almost every page (for example, still toward the end: "For me, death counts, it counts, and my days, my hours, and my seconds are numbered"). Let this posthumous volume be a token of how we will always remain in memory of him. That is to say, for life.

Laurent Milesi

Author's Note

H.C. for Life, That Is to Say . . ., the title first recalls a commitment, a promise, of course, the fiding [*fiance*] or trust in some given word ("it is for life," "for life and unto death"), the sharing of a friendship granted all life long: between Hélène Cixous and Jacques Derrida, ever since the encounter in Paris, some forty years ago, of two young professors and writers—both Algerian Jews from Algiers.

But *H.C. for Life, That Is to Say . . .* also records the taking of a side. Hélène Cixous took sides "for life." This is not an obvious thing to do, unlike what one might imagine. The side [*parti*] is also a wager [*pari*], an act of faith. What does it mean to wager one's life on life? What will the choice of life have meant for her? Not a "life-choice," but the side of life against death, for life without death, beyond a death whose test and threat are none the less endured, in mourning even in the life blood and breath, in the soul of writing. Where does this strange difference of opinion [*différend*] return from, this interminable "argument" between Jacques Derrida and Hélène Cixous, at the heart of their agreement, as to what death has in store deep within life itself, before the end? How can the latter stand *on the side* of life whereas the former feels drawn *to the side* of death? The answer to this question also depends on the meticulous analysis of the logic and topography of what is called a "side [*côté*]," of the recurrences of the word "side" in the lexicon of Hélène Cixous (alongside *cote* [quote, rating], *coté* [quoted, rated], *cotte* [coat], etc.) and of so many other words, for example, the wealth of the signifier *or* in the father's first name, Georges, the event of Eve in the mother's first name, or the mighty power of "might" [*la puissance de "puisse"*]—which leads to a big theoretical confrontation with Freud and his theory of the "omnipotence [*toute-puissance*]" of thought.

H.C. for Life, That Is to Say . . . could also be read as memoirs. At least as a part [*partie*] greater than itself, a measure without measure, a score [*partition*] rather, both sensible and decisive, of the memories of the author, Jacques Derrida. Indeed, as they take the form of a philosophical and, occasionally, philological account, of an anamnesis that is as scholarly as it is argued, these memoirs delve and search for their identity in the crypts of the past as much as in the vast work of Hélène Cixous. For it is an honest tribute that Jacques Derrida wants to pay to the thought of the woman whom he regards as one of the great French poets and writers.

Indeed, through many recollections but, above all, while meticulously, analytically, and carefully relying on so many admired texts by Hélène Cixous, on her desperate love of language, the poetics of her verbal inventions, her still unheard-of vocabulary, her inspiration and her punctuation, Derrida recalls what, during almost forty years, his friendship for her was like, the interminable reading of her work, their silent but endless conversation about the meaning of, for example, "believing," "might," "living" and "dying," etc. The friendship, the reading, the complicities of a silent altercation share without sharing but do not allow themselves to be separated. The one assigns the other for life, the two summon each other in the end: a final appointment, for another day, at the parting of ways to come.

H. C. FOR LIFE,
THAT IS TO SAY . . .

First I wish to express my gratitude to Mireille Calle-Gruber: for everything, for allowing me to speak first, in the first place, and for giving me the time to do so, all this given time, in the second place. It is an immeasurable privilege, and alas I myself could not possibly live up to it.

And I thank you all while already asking for forgiveness, at the same time, for the same given time, as well as for the patience that will be asked of you.

Prelude

At the moment of beginning, even before beginning, slowing down, *adagio* and even *lento, lento,* one knows, yes one knows that one will always have to begin again.

That is to say deploy or multiply the beginnings.

Which will be each time unique.

I will always have to begin again. As I will explain, there would even be a kind or genre of palinode about these rebeginnings, these reversions and retractions. Today I will only recall a series of possible beginnings. And very slowly at first. Do not become too impatient in the beginning, facing somebody who seems to become paralyzed on the threshold, who dares neither knock nor ring the bell, as if he were waiting in front of the door for it to slightly open by itself. It is as if it were to open by itself miraculously.

As for me, I keep forever reminding her each time, on my side, that we die in the end, too quickly. And I always have to begin again.

For she—because she loves to live—does not believe me. She, on her side, knows well that one dies in the end, too quickly; she knows it and writes about it better than anyone, she has the knowledge of it but she believes none of it. She does not believe, she knows; she is the one who knows and who tries, but she believes none of it.

And I say to myself, on my side: "Would that I might [*puissé-je*] believe her, I wish I *might* [puisse], yes, I wish I might believe her, where she believes none of it, when I say to her that one dies in the end, too quickly."[1] Or else, I say to myself: "Would that I *might* understand, I wish I *might* think what to believe means on her side, on the side where I am not. (Note that already I keep talking about her *side*.) That is to say that she should teach me what I mean when I say, 'I wish I *might* what I cannot.'" I cannot, but in saying "I wish I *might*," without really knowing if I think what I am saying, and what "to think what one says" means, well, in saying, "I wish I *might* believe her," or else, "Oh *if only* I could believe her, if . . . ," well, yes [*si*] maybe, maybe it is *as if* [comme si] I believed her already, yes, and if I could, and so she was indeed right—and I wrong in saying and repeating, on my side, because I love living too: "We die in the end, too quickly."

And it begins again. Again and again. It is magic, a singular, almost interminable argument. On which subject, basically?

Maybe it is better for me, even before beginning, to touch on some questions that will run through what I am going to say to you, because I will not have the time to develop them or even explain them, and barely enough time to ask them. All the time I wonder within myself about the phrase I have just pronounced ("Would that I might believe her," "I wish I might believe her"), what the meaning of this *subjunctive* may well be, of course,

"would that I might," "that I might," but above all how this subjunctive may be heard when it comes back to itself (just as a subject comes round to itself, to regain consciousness and wake up to
itself), when the first-person subjunctive of this verb wakes up to
what it is, potentially, *after* the detour of believing ("would that I
might believe her," "ah, make it so that I *might* believe her"), which
is also a detour through *her* ("believe her:" *là*).[2] The word "believe"
is most enigmatic and most equivocal. Its meaning changes in
French, it leaps beyond itself more briskly than many a word, from
one mode to another according to the syntagms that the idiom
readily accepts. For instance, I may "believe something": I may believe the weather will be fine in a moment,[3] whether I hope so or
not, and what I believe then may well be *possible*; but without believing something, I may also believe what someone tells me—for
instance that the weather will be fine in a moment, whether I hope
so or not, and what I believe then may well be *possible*. These first
two beliefs, even if they seem to have the same object, a certain
"in-a-moment" [*tout-à-l'heure*] of which we will have much more
to say, are certainly radically different: one works through the other's speech and the other does not. As for the other's speech, I can
believe it when it has to do with constative things (for instance,
the weatherman tells me in a forecasting mode: "The weather will
be fine in a moment"), but it is yet another mode of believing
when I must believe *in* the other's word, believe the other and take
his or her word for it; we are here dealing with a *believing* that has
to do with the act of faith in the given word. This *believing* that
believes in what the other says when he gives his word is radically
heterogeneous to the two previous ones. It seems then that the belief of the "believing *in* someone" is no less heterogeneous, beyond
all the beliefs I have just enumerated and even beyond the "believing in someone's word," in such and such a "given word." Not all
languages have one single word, as French does, for all these different meanings and uses of the word "believe." This apparent homonymy between so many verbs meaning "to believe" that mean
such heterogeneous things could be interpreted as a limitation or
as a chance in the French language. As a chance because, through

a certain untranslatability (homonymy is the royal way of the untranslatable itself, and therefore of cryptography: such will be the axiom underlying the whole of my argument), this homonymy gives us to think what "believing" may mean, at the bottom of the abyss. But I did not want to impose on you a lecture on the brink of abyssal belief. Simply I was interested in what happens when "believe" is preceded by this subjunctive (*would that* I *might*, that I *might, would that* we *might, would that* you *might* believe), which seems to play between the possible and the impossible. Absolute belief is only truly itself, tends toward its proper extremity, toward the *eskhaton* of its *eschatology*, where it does not believe only what is possible, and where it is possible to believe. If I believe the weather will be fine in a moment, whether someone tells me so or not, and if I know this may well be possible, this belief is hardly a belief; it is already a calculation, a weather forecast that reckons with probabilities. It is then possible and therefore easy to believe: therefore I do not need to believe in the strong sense of this word. The strong sense, the *mighty* sense of this word, therefore wakes up to itself when the matter or the cause of the belief (*what, in what, whom, in whom* I believe) no longer belongs to the order of the possible. To believe when it is possible and measurable only by the yardstick of the possible, is not yet to believe. If one hears the full might of meaning this word has, to believe should then lie and only reside in this impossible faith in the impossible. Then one could believe only in miracles. And to believe *would be* the miracle, the magical power of the miracle. The miracle would be the ordinary of belief. A belief agrees with, allies itself to, and promises itself to only the incalculable. If it were so, what would "would that I might believe" or "I wish I *might* believe" mean then? What does this subjunctive become? How would the mighty powers of this unbelievable belief in the impossible watch over what is called so glibly the fiction of a so-called literary event, over all that complies with the modality of a certain "as if"? And as each art entertains a different experience of fiction and therefore of belief, one may wonder what happens to believing and to the "would that I might believe" when arts graft, haunt, and mingle with one another. Music, for example. What about music in this respect? Supposing it also calls upon some belief (which is much more difficult to believe than for representational or narrative arts, let alone discursive arts in general), what happens when music becomes the very body of another art, of literature for instance? What happens to belief then? When one hears a piece of music, if one can hear it, for instance a song [*chant*], an "enchanting chant [*enchant*]," as is said in a text about magical enchantment, a hymn or incantation of which we will have more to say, then one believes or one no longer needs to believe in the same way as someone who would only hear the words of a narrative (whether fictional or not). What happens then, as far as belief and the impossible are concerned, when the song of the enchanting chant [*chant de l'enchant*] can no longer be dissociated from the whole body of words and from what still presents itself as the literality of literature? When literature becomes an enchanting chant?

Let us carry on as if I were abandoning these questions here.

....

I-met-her-some-thirty-five-years-ago-maybe.

And although I have probably never understood anything about it, although I have not understood her yet, we have probably never been apart. It is *as if* we had *almost* never been apart.

Yes, I believe, I-met-her-some-thirty-five-years-ago-maybe.

I would like to say and repeat this sentence as if it were a single, very long word, a single voiced unit, as if I were uttering it in tongues, unintelligibly, in a single breath.

She had written, she had written to me.

Before that, she has since told me, many long years before that, some seven years before, she had seen and heard me—but from behind.

She had seen and heard me, from behind, speaking. Facing an academic jury, as I was giving a presentation on the thought of death.[4] From the cathedral height of this jury of which he was already a member, Maurice de Gandillac could therefore have seen both of us at the same time. He was facing both of us, who were not facing each other. He remains at Cerisy the only witness who would have been entitled to this viewpoint: he could claim to have seen us together, virtually, to have caught us in his field of vision and seen us both coming, facing him, whereas we did not know each other and had never seen or heard each other face-to-face yet. I am sure Maurice de Gandillac's mind was elsewhere; he was probably thinking of something else and he missed that, but still, all this already belonged to the predestinal time of this château here at Cerisy—which thus became beforehand the name of our gathering in presence, at the end of this millennium, for which I once again wish to thank our hosts and Mireille. Here we are all together. This presence gathered unto itself, this parousia, could be given the name, after Hegel's fashion, of *paroucerisia* of absolute knowledge when it mocks everything, in particular God's death.

Which way for (the *paroucerisia* of) Cerisy? This way, of course [*Paroucerisie? Par ici bien sûr*].[5]

Note that in French *par ici* is an unheard-of expression, if you think about it; I hold it to be almost untranslatable, like the entire work of which we are going to speak, and wherever she speaks or utters the monosyllable *si* [if, yes], for instance, or "six,"[6] untranslatable too, like the unrepresentable or improbable conjunction of this preposition, this adverb, and this numeral, untranslatable like this very crossing of a "through" through a "here" [*la traversée même de "ici" par "par"*]. But untranslatable and unavowable too through the uninterrupted sketching of a parricide. I do say the sketching of a parricide, and its fiction, that of a *quasi*-parricide, a parricide in *if* or in *as if* [*en si ou en comme si*]. Here is a thesis on translation and on the "that is to say" that I will not have the time to develop, at least fully, and so I propose instead the ellipsis of a dogmatic syllogism in three points:

1. Quasi-parricide is the condition of translation;
2. Translation always and only translates the untranslatable;
3. Therefore quasi-parricide remains the condition of the translation of the untranslatable.

From all sides—and I do mean from all sides—the present session will therefore already have been promised as in a dream, more than thirty-five years ago, the promise of a ceremony.

As for myself, on the date of our encounter, I had never seen her, I had never heard her and never read her.

Have I done so since?

What she had written to me, before our encounter, was not a true letter, no doubt, but a postcard, a very *hasty* word, from afar, from the provinces (from somewhere near Arcachon or Bordeaux, near Montaigne, I believe, where, if I am not mistaken, she used to teach some thirty-five years ago).

But what she wrote to me then, a postcard, something hasty by way of a letter, already spoke of nothing but letters, writing, and literature. This hasty message, like what followed, became for me mightily spectral: between perception, memory, phantasm, hallucination, auto-suggestion, as many categories that are subjected *around here* [par ici] to much turbulence.

Only after which, after which postcard, we soon met, I mean we literally met, face-to-face [*à la lettre et de face*], one fine morning, the venue: the Balzar. Some time later, I was reading the manuscript of what was to be called *Le Prénom de Dieu*,[7] her first book, which did not yet have a name (I'll come back to that in the end, for my last beginning), and I already wondered what was happening here, the landing in full flight or the take-off lights ablaze of an unheard-of speech, the appearance of an unidentifiable letter and literary object. What *is* this? I asked myself more or less. What is happening here? What is happening to me? What genre? Who could ever read this? Me?

So I'll have to come back to it, I said to myself.

This will have been so far, as a prelude, even before the first beginning, nothing but a date, the benediction of a date, some thirty-five years ago (in fact I was slightly less than thirty-five years of age myself, midway life's journey, and as I am speaking, or am about to speak, only of her and not of myself, not at all of myself, by all means and as far as possible, I today nevertheless pronounce and go through more than half of life). As I was saying, this only remains a date inscribed in the wood of a tree or on a flyleaf in order to begin before the beginning, something like that special "plea" or "prayer" on the ends of books that is called a *prière d'insérer* [author's note], or a newspaper page, or an appointment scribbled in a diary—what is called in French an *agenda*, that is to say, as the word indicates, things that remain to be done. *Agenda*, what *needs doing*, what one needs to learn how to do, that is to say, by hypothesis, to learn what *to do* means. In the same way as I was saying just now that I would like to learn what *to believe* means, and what one does when one believes, and what makes it possible for one to believe. To learn what *to believe* means, what *to do* means—and what *to make someone believe* involves. To learn it from her, of course, is the wish that gathers us today, as I will have tried to learn ever since I have known her. What would need doing would then also be for me to come back to this matter of a card, of a card about letters on literature—and what followed from that.

What is literature, *on her side*? And what is so glibly called literary fiction, let alone the fiction of literature, the "if" or the "as if" of literature? What does that become on *her* side?

What is the language of literature, from the shores and far from the banks whence she came [*loin des rives dont elle arrive*], shores and banks that are and are not the same as mine? To come back to this matter of a card, to follow again the cartography of these shores and sides [*de ces côtes et de ces côtés*], means that I must at once address you, speak to you about it again, of course, but while recalling, meditating, trying to understand, *within myself*, what has been happening [*arrivé*] here, ever since that encounter, if it has happened, what to the letter has happened. While trying to think here [*par ici*] what may well have happened and happened to me in the wake of this matter of a card about letters on literature and what followed from that.

Would I ever be capable of it? And worthy?

End of the prelude. Which does not mean that I am ready to begin. I will propose to you in truth—I begin to announce it again—only a palinodic and unending series of virtual beginnings. *Les Commencements*, as she says in the title of one of her books[8]—and to confess it all and lay my cards on the table, in spite of all these beginnings, I will not say a word, for lack of time, about some forty-five to fifty of her books. For lack of time but also deliberately, so as not to touch them before you and to leave them intact for you.

A palinode: this beginning with which I will now begin again was already written; it came before the other, before everything I have just said. And that began with a presentation of the title: *H.C. for Life*.

As you hear it, it advances like a pronounced title: *H.C. for Life*.

An *unpublishable* title, then. As soon as one saw it on paper, I said to myself, it would lose its vital breath, *that is to say*, since it is equivocal, as they say in English, it should give up its voice, its vocalism, and its vocation. It is the *C* that would be ruined by this publication, where the initial of the proper noun I am about to sing the praises of but also to interrogate in my own way, this letter *C*, which, at first, was merely the initial of a patronymic name, by chance, my chance, also resonates like a homonym or a homophone. (I will not speak about myself but I will probably only ever be able to speak of my chances, of chances of what comes and happens to me.) Why this homonym or homophone and therefore the irony of the untranslatable, of which I said that it always leads to the trace of some parricide? A parricide of which we should not hasten to believe we know what it is. Because *C*, in this unique idiomatic phrase that will remain forever French, "*c'est pour la vie*," is united, the time of an apostrophe, to the homophone of the copula *is*, *c'est* [it is]. It thus forms one body with the intertwined body around which, spinning, dancing, and sinking, the vertiginous history of all philosophy, of knowledge, and of the question (*ti esti*) of Greek Europe has played itself out. Even before Plato, and not far from a certain Gorgias, whom I will bring back later. What is this? But also, what is this *C*? Who is she? Who is C? [*Qui est-ce? Qui est C?*] If one must always begin again, it is also because she herself gives about a thousand answers to this question, in speaking, as she says herself, through the six hundred voices that come to her. Keep in mind the syllable *si*, the phoneme or the musical note *si* [B], and six, the number six hundred, beyond what I am going to say about it just now.

I mentioned Greek Europe in passing, for we are probably also going to speak of the seas and oceans that separate the shores of that Occident from some other continents, even from some other occidents. And we will also have to speak of the mighty power of a thought, or of a word, "might [*puisse*]," which in advance eludes the "it is." Just as a certain performative eludes the constative and a certain subjunctive the indicative. Hélène Cixous's work is also, from these shores and abysses, the thousand-eyed witness, the voice with the "six hundred voices" that speaks of itself/herself at the end of *OR*, of itself/herself [*d'elle-même*][9] and of the letters of which she says, in an undecidable tense, that she had thought she would end by not reading them, that she will end by not reading them, not letting us know if, *in the end*, she will have read them. So I will read her, but trembling, having never read her aloud in public and without knowing where to pitch my voice, nor hers, nor her many voices for that matter, since she has got at least six hundred of them. Which is the one, masculine or feminine, of these six hundred voices, that weaves and braids all the others in unique fashion? I do not know. I read:

> Now I am alone with my near dead ones / deaths [*mes proches morts*].

"My near dead ones / deaths"—we will never know if they are her dead or her deaths, her near dead ones or deaths: untranslatable.[10]

> Now I am alone with my near dead ones / deaths. I had always thought that I would end by not reading these letters. They may well be so without arms [*si sans bras*; a homonym or homophone of "six hundred" in the next sentence—JD] without a frown. I believe I was afraid of their six hundred voices. They were so much more numerous than the taciturnities of my father inside, my reel father-face [*père bobine*] my wo-man [*hommefemme*] to whom I owe my beginnings my old enchanter.[11]

I have just said that, in speaking of her and in asking myself, "What is it?" or "Who is it?" I will only have meditated, through the throw of the dice of this title, on my own chance. My chance, just like H.C., is linked to that which in "H.C. for life" remains untranslatably French. The equivocal vocation of this title speaks only French; one might as well say that it provokes a translation it defies, forevermore. I dare say, in a word, even before I begin again, that this is true, to a hyperbolic degree, of the whole work of H.C. One pattern of her destiny might in fact be intimately linked with this history of translation and transference. And therefore with her (hi)story of the French language. The provocative call for an impossible translation cannot but provoke accordingly at the same time, together with the unavowable desire, admiration, and transference, transferential resistances to reading and strategies of avoidance in the very act of acknowledgment or recognition, which I would like to try and analyze later, at least in its principle.

To say that the title *H.C. for Life* cannot bear publication or at least readability, that it must remain audible but unreadable; and then to say that, even if audible, it must not become visible because that would be too unbearable, because it would fall flat and cease to breathe from being grammatically exposed to the gaze, naked in the body of its letter, where it cries out first and foremost to be heard; does this really mean that the unpublishable, here, the nonpublic, belongs to the reserve of the private or to the intimacy of the secret, as if this title had to remain a password among us, such as we may be, whichever genre/gender or name one may grant (to agree with) such and such?

Maybe—one should not swear to it—one must or can never rule it out. But what I am attempting to approach today, through "H.C. for life," a phrase by which I decide to name, inseparably, someone, man or woman, *and* something we call her work, at once its signatory, her signature, *and* what she signs, is an arch-secret *and* arch-public place, which, consequently, nullifies what it makes possible, namely the distinction between the public and the private, the phenomenal and the secret, the readable and the indecipherable of an absolute crypt. *L'Histoire qu'on ne connaîtra jamais*, the title of this recent play, becomes—and this is true for each of her titles—the metonymy of everything.[12] This nullification of the border, this passage of the forbidden between the public and the private, the visible and the hidden, the fictional and the real, the interpretable and the unreadable of an absolute reserve, like the collusion of all genres, I believe, is at work at every moment. It is the very work of her writing, its operation and its opus, which, although literary through and through, also goes beyond literature, just as it goes beyond autobiography. And my hypothesis will be that the excess and surplus of this passage precisely passes through *life*, a word that becomes all the more obscure. It passes through the mighty powers of which one can say, as I will try to explain: "It is for life," through the "for" as much as through the "life" of this "for life."

"H.C. for life" is therefore a label that is at once controlled (an "*appellation contrôlée*," as they say in the Bordeaux area) and uncontrollable as soon as you hear it pronounced. The appellation of an appeal pronounced because here I am uttering it and pronouncing it and want it pronounced. I insist that it remain pronounced. Pronounced also in the sense of "decided," resolved, clearly marked, accepted, characterized. Articulated by a voice that is not afraid of words even if it is afraid of all the rest and never manages to hear itself, that is to say, to hear everything that is being said or that it intends to say. A title of appeal, then, that is not oracular but resolute and resolutely *oral*—a word that allows me to speculate on gold [*or*] and the *aura* of what passes only by word of mouth to the ear, between *os* and *aures*. Under the golden sign of this aurality, I would like to salute a work whose writing never gives up on itself (it is the most written writing there is), while doing justice to the gold of orality for its most inventive virtue, giving and dipping into its priceless and ageless resources, the ones that are most deeply buried and most archaic, in so many languages, but which are also the most reserved for and through the future-to-come [*avenir*] of a work.[13]

I do not know any work—if I say of the twentieth century, it is out of a sense of propriety and politeness, but I am not even sure and I would not swear to it—I, for my part, have never read anything produced in the twentieth century that comes from a place where the most powerfully calculated writing, the polyphonic composition from the grain of the voice to the amplitude of songs, the formal and so punctuated goldsmithery of the signs on the page, and the rhythms of the textual body, become thus allied—a watchful and deliberate strategy, an impeccable vigil—to the most spontaneous living breath of the word as voiced (of the oral signifier before and through the word, of the word voiced before and beyond the verbal), where both the waking and dreaming (just like, a moment ago, the public and the private, the fictional and the real, the phantasmatic and the actual, and like all the genres) do their utmost and manage to cross their own boundaries, to push their limits, and to provoke the reader. To provoke the reader into awakening: analyze, scrutinize yourself along this line, this lineage, the thin edge of this passage between the public and the secret, between waking and dreaming, between fiction and reality, between the credible and the incredible, between such and such a literary or dramatic genre, between this sexual gender and another, that is to say, so many other limits still that we are going to try to acknowledge or recognize. Acknowledging/recognizing while avoiding them once more, according to a word that awaits us, a word of Freud's and/or Hélène Cixous's, his great-niece.

A title is often an announcement, the effect of an announcement or an annunciation. Here I am thinking of the pronouncement of a pronunciation rather: *H.C. for Life*, uttered before and beyond any visibility and therefore any readability. It is a question of speaking to the ear, and the ear alone, where it does not know yet how to read. Hence, sometimes, the necessity for me to write down some of these words on the board. To speak, therefore, where there still remains something to learn: how to read and live, for life—up to the end.

As you have already realized, I might have to be eschatological. Out of habit but also as an exception. The *eskhaton* or the ultimate, the last, the end up to the end, the extreme, sometimes the verdict of a Last Judgment, is by definition an absolute exception, even grace maybe, that which one cannot turn into a habit, first because one no longer has the time to do so. The *eskhaton*, that is to say, what one can no longer reappropriate for oneself, and which therefore resists any form of *habitus*.

Eschatologically, I will therefore speak extremely about extremes, that is to say, about what starts finishing or ends up beginning—that is to say, about who comes first for the last, for the last time, and about what it means to be the last man or woman (besides, *dernier*, in French, is untranslatable; a fictitious word, *derrenier*, reconstructed from *deretranus*, from *de retro*—from the rear, from behind, back to front, conversely; *retro vivere*, as Seneca says about life lived against the trend of others), the first becoming the next to last of life and death, the one before the rearmost [*l'avant-derrenier*] of what comes first and last. *Derrenier*—what a word, isn't it? It will guide us much later, last, where one could say, there, *in the last instance*, toward the re(ar)-denial of a re(ar)-negation [*le* dé-renier *d'un* dé-reniement], of a renegation which in reneging or denying itself will complicate the logic of simple denial and the laws of resistance or avoidance as well as those of acknowledgment.[14] In this evident avoidance of the event you can already hear, as in a dream, the first name of a mother, both hers and ours, the Eve of humanity.

For example, as I was saying, why me? Why should I be the first and not the last to speak here? I say "for example" because all this would be said "for example," as if I were going to remind people all the time that I am speaking of one of H.C.'s works, for example: for example *La*, this unheard-of title, that is to say, infinitely equivocal. For very obvious reasons, I would not be able to do what I should because that would take more than a lifetime. So, for example, why should I be *here* the first to speak, *here*? But *here* is always an example and therefore another here, *there*, elsewhere, already, yesterday and tomorrow. Philosophy begins with *there* [*commence par* là]—see the first dawn of any phenomenology of the mind: thinking begins by taking account of the fact that, as soon as I say *here*, and especially if I write it, *here* is no longer *here*, *around here* [par ici], but already *there* [là], around there [*par là-bas*], elsewhere, on the *other side*; and *I is another*, another I, me and wholly other I.[15] Then the deictic gets carried away, the finger shows and "monsters" [*ne montre et ne monstre*] only when it begins to journey and to travel, if only through the memory of itself. But why would I have been here [*par ici*] the first to speak about Hélène Cixous?

I ask myself whether I should not rather be the rearmost [*derrenier*] to be able to speak of her, the last to know how to speak of her, to be able, if only through a pronounced title, to pronounce myself, to pronounce on her, her thought, and her work.

And yet it is true that someone in me, one of me, is still dreaming about being the first to speak of her, that is to say, to announce her, to predict, to say to those who have not yet seen her that she is coming, that she has already come, and that she has not been recognized yet.

As if I were destined to be her prophet. Not her announcer, nor her impresario for a number or act, the number or character she *is* or the number she *calls* or *performs* (you will recognize that number later as a circus number—the flying trapeze, for example—or as a telephone number). As if I were destined around here to be not the impresario or the showman of her number but her prophet.

As if I had heard or seen her before the others and were coming to say, inheriting the rightful anger of certain prophets who address their people: what on earth are you waiting for to see and hear her? Beware the wrath of history—or of God, if you prefer.

As if I had seen or heard her, read her before the others, as I was saying. Well, it is this "as if" that I will be putting to excessive use. And through the fiction of this "as if," for the time given to me, but as if I had a whole life before me, more *as if*, even more on the *as if*, I would like to tell you, with all the naïveté I am capable of, how I discovered H.C.; the time and place of our first encounter, some thirty-five years ago; my first reading of the first manuscript of her first book, *Le Prénom de Dieu*. For everything seems to have begun then, with the time of *Le Prénom de Dieu*. I will not be able to do much more than sketch or anticipate, as a dotted outline, the interminable conference lecture or the interminable confession that I dreamed of imposing on you. I would have wished to invent, for the occasion of addressing Hélène and in her honor, a new genre or gender [*genre*] and a new name for this new genre or gender, beyond all the differences or rather by playing on all the differences, something in between the whispered confidence of the confessional and the authority of the philosophical, theoretical, critical, or poietic conference lecture, a portmanteau word for Cerisy, between confession, confidence, and conference. But all this will remain deferred for so many reasons; it will remain inchoate, preliminary, on the edge, *on the side*, in the imminence of the immensity to which I would have liked to accord today a new Encomium of Helen, worthy of making the manes of Gorgias jealous. Maybe I will nevertheless have the time to renew *up to the moment* [tout à l'heure], but much later, this *Gorgiou Elenes Egkômion*—Gorgias' chant to Helen's glory—by citing it. Everything will remain just like this God of the beginning, this God of God's Forename, barely named, prenamed, initialed and initialized. . . . [16]

I will merely initial(ize) "H.C. for life"; I will merely initialize, as one says these days in the code of word processors, the program or the software with the unprogrammable thing in sight that one day, during the time and life I might still be given, I would like to say and which needs to be written in a way that is commensurate with the person and the work that have brought us together here.

"H.C. for life."

That is to say what? Who is this? It is first of all, therefore, a pronounced title. After having pronounced it, I believe that I judged it, during the time of an endless remorse, to be unpronounceable.

I do not know whether, more than her, sooner than her, better than her, anyone will have ever given me to think what *to live* means. Not that she taught me how to live—that is not the same thing, and it could sometimes resemble its exact opposite, I mean "learning how to die." Not that in giving me to think what to live might mean, she assured me that living meant something, something in relation to which thought and knowledge would go hand in hand and would grant us something, giving us over to something firm and reassuring. No, giving me to think what amounts to living even beyond any will-to-say [*vouloir-dire*], beyond any "that is to say," and maybe even beyond any will, beyond a living or a life that would still depend on a will, a will-to-live [*vouloir-vivre*], and even a power-to-live [*pouvoir-vivre*], beyond any knowledge, any power, and any contradiction, for example between living and dying. I feel that all this is obscure and I ask for forgiveness. In a moment [*tout à l'heure*], starting from her texts, I will explain myself better. But I wished from the beginning to allow for this feeling of obscurity, of night, and of initial incomprehension, in places where I probably have not understood her.

This pronounced title had been dictated to me. By which I mean breathed out, at once the inspired spirit, inspired from the depths whence life comes, life *for life*, life promised to life, the animation of *anima, ruah*, the breath of life, the heart and the soul, and just as soon stolen, furtively withdrawn, one day on the telephone.

I would have liked to keep talking to you, to keep you on the telephone. In the beginning, there will have been the invention of the telephone. Magic and technique. There will have been the telephone. We know it. Between the lines of what we have been writing, for decades, that is to say, for people of our generation, throughout a whole lifetime, between so many lines of writing, there will probably have been the unique infinity of a telephone line. If there were a conceivable, acceptable statistics, whether dream or reality, on this subject, I do not know to what comparative archive it would give rise with regard to the respective number of words pronounced, words that we all of us here have addressed to one another. Without being capable of this calculation, I am sure that someone or other among us can tell: we have spoken with each other on the telephone more than alone together—face-to-face, as they say. Infinitely more. So it may no longer be an original situation today for so many of us in this very place. But this shared situation puts us on the wireless line of the telephone,

even before being "*on line*," as they say nowadays, and it gives us
to think what a line is and what it is not when it describes a certain line between those who, as is the case, are devoted to the line
of writing—and even, as is her case, in a writing that is entirely oc-
cupied by generation, filiation, the lineage of writing—devoted to
the work as lineage. As I will often have to do, I leave aside here, in
passing, what could be the program or title of some ten or twenty
academic theses to come, tomorrow, when the university has no
choice but to canonize the corpus of H.C. Subject: telephones and
the question of the telephone in the work of H.C. I give some references but will not do so each time. I will speak a lot more about
the telephone—it is here everywhere with her, down her way [du
côté *de chez elle*][17]—and I will tell you how she speaks *on* or *to*
the telephone, but here is already, to begin with the beginnings, a
reference for whoever would like to take note: long before *Messie*
(1996), from which a huge hymn to the telephone arises, not to
AT&T but to T.I.T. (Tristan and Isolde on the Telephone), there
was *Les Commencements* (1970). A voice writes this History with
a capital:

> I could also write the History of the telephone and how we tamed
> it. . . . [18]

Would that you might read *everything* that precedes and *everything* that follows, as you should each time I cite or "quote," for
example this word "tamed."[19] As this project of a History of the
telephone is pronounced at a distance but in the vicinity of Saint
Georges, you would find there, tamed or not, all the animals from
Uccello's painting *Il Drago*, the serpent and the lion, but also step-
by-step a certain telephonic elephantasm that will also be made
to wait patiently, like a well-behaved elephant. One day one will
write about the animals, all these living creatures that her writing
welcomes, for life—to the letter and in thought, beyond simple
domestic hospitality and beyond philosophy. "My greatest difficulty is to move from my menagerie to philosophy," says a voice
in *Messie* in a telephone scene with Abraham's donkey on Mount
Moriah.[20]

So "H.C. for life" was a pronounced declaration—on the telephone—when Mireille Calle-Gruber ordered me to provide her without delay with a title ready for publication, quite a long time ago, even before I had the slightest idea what I was going to say to you today. I only knew that I would be the first to speak. Thus the most exposed, the firstborn sacrificed by the princely privilege conferred upon him. Sacrificed unless pardoned / to less than a grace [*à moins d'une grâce*]. One has to take the angel into account but never count on him.

A pronounced declaration, then. That is to say what? What does "pronounced" signify here? This would designate a declared declaration—decided, of course, marked, insistent, signed, accepted, deliberate, a declaration leaning declaredly and squarely to one side rather than another.

But "pronounced" means something else, above all: "pronounced" means to *say* and not *write*, means to say before writing, wants to say before letting itself be written. "Pronounced" wants to say, and not write, what allows itself to be heard before allowing itself to be read, what is uttered before being lined up and couched on the page. For the *C* in H.C., if one hears it without seeing it, if one lends an ear before reading, is also *c'est* [that is], that is to say [*c'est à dire*], to be heard verbally as a verb, *c'est*, the verb of the basic predicative clause (subject, verb, complement or object). Here one knows [*on sait*] that the *c'est* agrees with knowledge. The formidable task, the one that I am afraid of, because I am afraid of her, the dangerous experimentation, the experilous experience awaiting me, is to put into question the *C* of *c'est*, its present indicative of the verb *être* [to be], in the name of another modality, in the name of the subjunctive of another verb, while avoiding wounding the *C* of her proper noun, which I would like to celebrate instead.

Here is another beginning now, so I change beginnings as one changes gear.

"The letters of omnipotence [*toute-puissance*]" is a quotation.

Hers are letters of omnipotence. They arrive, they are made to arrive. If one is to believe her.

Her own, her letters.

How should one hear and understand that? In what sense would these letters be *of omnipotence*? In what sense would they be her letters, her own? Her own because she writes them, intends them for a destination, and, precisely, addresses them? Or else her own because the other addresses them to her and she, precisely, knows how to receive them, or to send them to herself as their destination? Among so many addresses, this is a distinction that the afore-said omnipotence, precisely, abolishes.

For one should renew, take the risk, for her, and I will later take the risk of renewing, that is to say, reinventing a word like "might."

What is this word, "*might*"? What would this word, all fresh and new-minted, maybe yet unheard-of, be? Whence would it thus come, unrecognizable, a homonym only to itself? If one follows the secret of homonymy in all its guises, which will be one of my leads, how can one track down this deceitful double of the old word "might," whose familiar traits we believe we can recognize in the big family, one should say in the *dynasty* of the *dynamis*, of power, of the dynast, of the possible and of potentiality? Whence would this yet unknown word "*might*" come, whose resurrection I would like to dedicate to her, first by giving it back to her, for it is her own, newly minted? Like the very *event* whose mighty power is always might—which makes something come, come about, happen, or arrive.

To give back to her later, but scarcely recognizable, this word (of) "might," I will not be on her side. I will not speak from/of her side [*de son côté*]. Nor from/of mine anyway. We will have to ask ourselves, much later, what being on someone's side, on the other's side, also means. But also at the other's side. Or else alongside the other, which does not amount to the same thing.

In everything I myself will say today, I will not be on her side. This may be the condition for me to attempt to speak of her or to her. If I were on her side, I could not speak of her nor tell her any-thing whatsoever. Nor especially receive anything whatsoever from her. Not the slightest grace. I am therefore not on her side.

Unless—and this is a hypothesis we cannot rule out, alas, nei-ther you nor I—I manage neither to speak to her nor precisely to speak of her, neither to receive from her nor to recall her, if I may say so, because I remain too much on her side. There is a risk, which will remain suspended up to the end, and probably beyond, that I may remain powerless to say anything worthwhile for any-one. For even though I have chosen not to stand on her side here, I am sure neither to be on mine nor what "shore" [*côte*], "bank," and "side" [*côté*] mean here. If I were on her side, I could not say anything of her nor to her, but I could not see anything coming from her any better. And I cannot be reconciled to that idea. As I accumulate the false steps and false starts to begin with, I will say at least that not only do I no longer know which side I am on and from which side I am about to speak (neither from hers nor from mine), not only do I no longer know what a side is (for example, as they say, the side of life or the side of death), but above all I do not know whom I name or call when I say "she" or "her." How to speak of her? How not to do so? How to avoid her?

Hélène Cixous, as they call her, as she is called, that's her. But is it her, Hélène, my friend in life, for life, Hélène who is here before us and among us? Or else her homonym Hélène Cixous, as they call her, the signatory author of an immense work whose name and fame resound throughout the world, the address, origin, and destination of so many letters of omnipotence of which I am just about to speak? As for her name, her family name or patronymic, her author's name, we spoke about it, even debated it, very soon after our first encounter some thirty-five years ago. Then I did not even know her maiden name, basically, I did not know her father was called Georges Cixous, and, while I sensed it maybe, I certainly did not know consciously that the *or* hidden in this first name, Georges, would give rise, up to its most recent revolution, only last year, to one of the most singular and inventive, alchemi-cal, and metonymic transmutations of our times, one of the most

powerful and thoughtful even, that I know in the history of literature—from Georges, the first name of a narrator in one of the
short stories in *Le Prénom de Dieu* (1967) to the Saint Georges of
Les Commencements (1970) to Jeor in *Portrait du soleil* (1973), and
so many other substitutes, including the golden letters *or* hidden
in so many words and so many letters in *OR* (1997). At the time
[*lors*] of our first encounter, she had hardly published anything
yet—and nothing under this name: H.C., Hélène Cixous. If we
had the time, I would speak to you about that again. She did not
yet know under what family name to publish. Already on that
point, as regards her author's name, we were not on the same side.
And already I had not understood her.

She herself: Who is she? Where is she, from one homonym to
the other, from one pseudonym to the other? Which side is she
on? In order to adjust my speech ever so slightly, knowing that
in any case I would not be able to live up to the vast scope of this
work here, I should at least choose, unilaterally, one of these homonyms and pretend to know what a "side" means.

I probably will not make things simpler by saying that, on this
subject as well, I am going to cite (*quote*) her right now and let her
speak, let her reply, hear her give one of her six hundred possible
replies to this question *on the side*—and the question of knowing
which side she herself is on, in order to try and find out where to
put myself, in this very place, and to which side I must hold. In
letting her speak, without knowing whom I am letting speak, I
will perform a gesture that I warn you I will multiply almost with
every sentence, powerless as I am to deal with my subject consistently and to live up to a work whose very *element* is a brilliant and
impregnable provocation, which turns each of its atomic elements
into a part greater than the very element, namely the whole, the
middle, the comprehensive set, the metonymico-atomic element
that comprises all the elements. Besides, I have just rediscovered
for her and have begun to love otherwise the word "ele*ment*." "Ele-
ment" may be one of the best words to sum up her work in one
word, a word that resembles her: element, *elementa*, in Latin, are
letters, literal atoms of writing, the *stoikheia* of which the Greek

Atomists Plato and Aristotle speak, but also the principles, the elements of sciences, and also, as principles precisely, the four elements that make up and contain the whole of being [*étant*], of the *physis* or of *cosmos*, fire, water, earth, air or the psychical breath, the spirit or the soul of life. Well, first of all, her work in my eyes is *elemental* (ele*ment*: earth, between silencing and lying [*terre, entre taire et mentir*]) in both these senses and in all these senses. It is made up of letters (*stoikheia, elementa*), each of which is greater than the whole, that is, mightier than the element that comprises it. Furthermore, and maybe above all, I love this word, element, to designate this work, which I read as naturally I breathe,[21] which I read [*lis*] and forget [*oublie*] and forgetread [*oublis*] all the time, according to what she calls *oublire* at the beginning of *OR*,[22] a work that I have known as much as I have failed to know and been ignorant of almost forever. This work remains for me all the more difficult to think and present since it is, on my side, elemental, the element of the element. And the question that will always remain impossible for me is, between these two nouns ending in -*ment*, *élément* and *événement* [event], the question of knowing how an event can happen to the element. Where there is an element, is it not impossible that there might be an event? But the final -*ment* in these two words, between *elle* [her] and Eve, may carry the whole burden of proof and truth, between the dreamed and the evident.

Powerless to clarify simultaneously the cosmic play of each literal element, which is always greater than the pan-cosmic element, powerless to relate everything incessantly to everything else, like a sorcerer's apprentice in pyrotechnics who would do his utmost in order to make light, to ignite each word through contact with all the others, not a faulty contact but a genuine contact with all the words that this word magnetizes in the work in progress, without risking inflaming the whole in a general short circuit, I have found no other solution than to go slowly, *lento*, where she herself goes so fast, *allegro, presto*, to proceed, elementally, grammatically, from station to station, that is to say also from digression to digression, from false start to false start, leaving the possible echo regularly suspended—or leaving the *mèche* alight (which in French can refer to the wick of a pilot light, the fuse of a time bomb, or, as you will see, a lock of hair), the *mèche* of each of my remarks, as if I were constantly telling you: here, you see, I interrupt the contact and the reading; follow the *mèche*, I indicate a possible way for you, I locate the necessity of a study, of a program for decades beyond any *décade*,[23] the dream of a thesis or of a poem in six times six volumes, which I would have loved to write myself and read to you if you had had the time. But we do not have the time, at this pace.

In order to let her speak, either her or her, the homonym itself, Hélène Cixous or Hélène Cixous, her name or her first name, to hand over to her, on the side of the side, on the subject of the side *where* she is, wherever she may be, and to make you understand what I mean when I confess that I am neither on her side nor on mine and that I no longer know where to put myself, nor where to pitch my voice, this is what I discover, for example, in *Jours de l'an* (1990):

> It is as if someone said to us: your dead father, would you like it if he wasn't? I cannot look the answer in the face.
>
> One difference between the author and me: the author is the daughter of the dead-fathers. *I* am on the side of my living mother. Between us everything is different, unequal, rending.[24]

Who signs these lines? From which side? It is obviously the author, since we read this in a book. But this author is someone who says: "A difference between the author and me." So it is "me" who speaks and speaks of the author, but of the author who nevertheless speaks, since it is also the author of the book, of the difference between me and the author. And one of the two, "me" (but it is a "me" who, for the author, is another), the "me" for the author, the "me" according to the author, says: "*I* am on the side of my living mother."

Admire, moreover, would that you might admire, where I read too fast, the personal pronoun that put in place the very question. It is neither me, nor him, nor her, namely the author, it is *us*. Remember the question:

It is as if someone said to **us**: your dead father, would you like it if he wasn't? I cannot look the answer in the face.

The *us* that receives the question (a fictional question because it is an impossible question: "It is **as if** someone said to us . . . ," she says) is therefore at the same time the *us* of the two homonyms, the *us* of the two, the author and me, even "the two of us, us the children, my brother and me," or even the comprehensive *us*, which includes the reader, the personal pronoun of the first person plural, the author, every other, you *and* me, me standing here *beside* and *on the side* of my living mother, but me also, the author, the daughter of the dead-father*s*. This plural of the dead-fathers gives way to the substitution of the fathers: there are so many of them—and this plural affects simultaneously, like a single noun, a single hyphenated nominalized adjective, the dead-fathers (and not *my* dead fathers, but the daughter of the dead-father*s*: she says here *my* living mother and the dead-father*s*). Now this plural does not affect the dead-fathers as fathers and, a hyphen between the subject and the complement, the dead-fathers, the fathers who happen to be dead, no, it pluralizes through death; it is through death that the plural, therefore the substitution, comes from that side which is not a side; it is insofar as he is dead that the father is in the plural—there are fathers on account and as a result of death; it is the death of the father that brings about his replacement, and he is saved, saved from death, as we will see, only by saving his uniqueness through substitution, through the place taken, through the event, through the occurrence of the substitution, which happens here and which, *taking place*, takes the place in this empty element of replaceability; even though—a terrifying aporia, which is at work throughout—one also saves the father, the unique father, by replacing him according to the law of a substitution or of a metonymy, of an infinite metempsychosis. One saves the unique father in the sense that he is already haunted by another unique father, an alternative father [*un père bis*]. Note that in this book at least, and in this work of fiction among others, the author, who is also the author of this work of infinitely regenerative substitution, is presented as a *daughter* of the dead fathers, whereas it is not said about me that I am the *daughter* of my living mother, but only that I am on her *side*: "the author is . . . ," she says, "I am . . . " ("the author is . . . ," third person of the verb *to be*: the author *is, she is* the daughter of the dead-fathers), "I *am*" (first person of the verb *to be*: I am): "The author *is* the daughter of the dead-fathers. *I* am *on the side* of my living mother." Not the daughter of the living mother, because *it is* the author who is a daughter, and not the daughter of the father but of the fathers, in the plural, and of the dead-fathers; whereas *I*, who am therefore no longer a daughter, the daughter of the mothers nor even the daughter of my mother, I am *on the side* of *my* living mother. Living and unique. There are dead-fathers, there is only one living mother, she is irreplaceable, and though I am not her daughter, I am on her side. And she is mine, *my* living mother. For the possessive adjective suits the mother, not the father: the daughter of the dead-father*s is* the author, whereas *I* am *on the side* of *my* living mother. Nowhere, in this remarkable sequence at least, is there "my father." And I am not on the side of *my father*, nor of the fathers, but on the side of *my living mother*. This may be one of the differences between *Jours de l'an* and *OR*. For example. For, in *OR*, the father is named "*my* father" more than once. The possessive is even explicitly claimed and demanded:

> Until this morning I had never received a letter from my father. The one who from death comes back when I call is *my* father ["my" is then underlined as a possessive adjective, which, however, is nothing less than possessive.—JD], the one I pull out of myself from the shipwreck with deep mourning. He comes out of my waters soaked charming but has never left any trace when returning behind the curtain.[25]

My father is as much and as little mine, my own, as a child who comes out of me, whom "I pull out of myself" (birth is always a mourning followed by depression) and who comes out of my waters, soaked, as from an amniotic shipwreck. Oedipus is born, maybe, he is nothing but the mourning of his mother Antigone in this catastrophe of generations of which she is the great poet-priestess. Oedipus, that's her, his mother, that is to say, his Antigone.

What does that mean? A "side," that is to say what? Let us not forget we are dealing here with a fictional question in a work of fiction. Let us not neglect that surplus of evidence. The evidence is so glaring, and so is the avoidance of the evidence, that one risks forgetting it: in this overall fiction, the aforesaid "me" is a character as much as the "author," neither the one nor the other being Hélène Cixous who is here present, neither the one nor the other being on her side, where she will have played with the law and the meaning of this mad combinatory; even though we do know it, neither the author nor me is *her*, herself (what does "herself" mean in this whole metonymic chain?), nevertheless, neither the "author" nor "me," nor what she calls the "author" and "me" is *without* her, and one has to look again on her side, on the side of her name, in order to pose these questions, between literature and its other, fiction, the possible, the real, and the impossible.

I therefore recall once more this other evidence, which one risks losing on the way: inside the book's overall fiction, inside the fictional element, the question that opened this declaration ("the author is the daughter of the dead-fathers. *I* am on the side of my living mother") was also a fictional question, a fiction within fiction, *as if* in the *as if*, fiction to the power of two opened in fact by an *as if* ("It is as if someone said to us: your dead father, would you like it if he wasn't?"). A fictional or simulated interrogation. It is probably not a "*rhetorical question*," nor just literature, but *at once* a question that maybe says under what condition one enters literature and above all a question that rules out the answer, an intolerable question, an impossible question, whose answer she says she cannot look in the face.

But what is the impossible? The only possible questions are impossible questions. The possible questions are those to which one has the answer, those whose answers one can look in the face. These are not true questions. The only true questions are the impossible ones, those whose answers one cannot look in the face. And which therefore are not questions, since these questions, which however are the only true questions, are not possible questions.

What then is a question? A possible question or an impossible question? Since one could not answer this very question, the answer given here is certainly not the right one; it is the substitute of an answer, it takes the place of the answer that she cannot look in the face. The answer is therefore beside the point [*à côté*], side-stepping the issue [*d'un pas de côté*] in a way that stages what I will call the big scene of the side down her way [*du côté du côté de chez elle*].

Now what does "side" mean around here? "On her side" or "down her way" [*du côté de chez elle*]? Beyond a neutral topology, "to be on the side of" indicates the bias of someone who takes one side rather than the other, in a disagreement [*différend*] if not a pitched battle between two parties; to be on the side of is not necessarily to be located or to live down somebody's way. To be or not to be on her side does not signal in the direction where she lives [*du côté de chez elle*], not even of some house with an even number[26] on one side of Avenue Coty.

By insisting twice on the fictional nature of this text and these questions or answers as fictions within a fiction (first to mark that these are not *her* answers or *her own* actual theses and that one can, for each of these sentences, find a way to contradict her from another agency in another sentence of the same book or of another book from one of the six hundred voices), I did not merely want to say that her books belong to the *genre* of fiction, as is sometimes mentioned in bibliographies (distributed in the "by the same author" section into generic categories like short stories, novels, drama, fiction). If one takes seriously, as it seems to me one must, the canonical question of the poetics of literary genres in the case of this work, I would be tempted, and I'll come back to this later, time permitting, to question *all* these categories, and in particular, that of fiction. Although all these texts are transfixed with fiction, and with fiction to the nth power, the fictional element does not dominate, in the last instance, more than anything else does, whether it be called narrative, novelistic, dramatic, autobiographi-

cal. Her poetics runs through all that at the same time and something else. Her fictional hyperrealism poses to the classification of
modes and genres the most formidable, the most unheard-of, and
the most interesting problems.

The "side," then, that is to say what? Or who? I often ask myself
this question, wondering at the same time whether and why I am
not on her side nor have ever been (and what this means, as for
her, on her side), but first and foremost with regard to the strange
and insistent use that she herself makes, on her side, of the word
"side." Books would need to be written, and I will not do so, on
these words: "shore" or "rib" [*côte*], "rating" [*cote*], "coat" [*cotte*],
"quota" or "quote" [*quote*], "side" [*côté*], "at the sides" [*aux côtés*],
"beside" [*à côté*], "sideways" [*de côté*], and "on the side of her own
side" [*du côté de son côté à elle*]. What is a side?

Having reached this point, and still before beginning, I propose
to leave aside for a moment this question of the side; I promise
to return to it after a detour of a few minutes. This detour will
last the time of a quasi-methodological exercise meant to give you
an example, once and for all, of what I will not be able to do,
although I should, with each exploration, with each port of call
rather, on the coastal map that I am going to follow. Let us imagine a reading at the bottom of the elemental sea: the exploratory
movement of a diving submarine. With the shores in sight, one
would adjust a periscope from afar in order to have a commanding
view of the coastline while watching out for the floating minefield,
or even the volcanic subsoil, in any case for the magnetic seabed
above which one tries to orient oneself, as if unconscious, with the
vigilance of a submarine subconscious.

One would need to be aware at every moment, at every quotation, at every word, and demonstrate (which I could not do, for
lack of time in particular) that the whole work, some fifty books,
every one of them equally singular, is magnetized, held in high-
tension vibration, by the power of a magnetic subsoil at once actual and virtual, a bedrock that recharges each verbal unit with the
memory and the projection of all the others. Here is a single example then. We were just talking about this "question" whose answer

she cannot "look in the face," the one about "your dead-father," which she displaces into "daughter of the dead-fathers," and the side [*côté*] or the rib [*côte*] of Eve, her living mother. It is in *Jours de l'an* (1990), therefore twenty years after *Les Commencements* (1970). Now what happens in between the question and the answer, what is the event in question in *Les Commencements*, a book in which Saint Georges, let me remind you, is like the hero who speaks of a "fear of acknowledging the possibility of the impossible"?[27] Now it so happens that five pages later, later than this possibility of the impossible, the question about the question is already posed—with a force and a necessity that the philosophers who are experts in the question about the question would do well to meditate. Here, in order to be thought—and it is *thought*, according to me, in the most powerful sense of the word—the question about the question (and thus about the answer) is first posed, as always, to Freud, from Freud, and probably against Freud, her uncle Freud, "my nuncle Freud," Nuncle Freud, as he is called in another book. For Freud is one of her own kinsmen—you know that—like so many others, but probably an author-character-member of the family more permanent and insistent, even clinging (he never wants to leave), even closer than the others, from Kafka to Lispector, from Kleist to Tsvetayeva, from Rembrandt to Akhmatova, from Montaigne to Thomas Bernhard, or from Celan to Beethoven to Stendhal to God; Freud comes and goes everywhere, like an uncle by marriage, a beloved, well-known ancestor but one who is challenged and heckled in every way in a number of her books, with a degree of competence and vigilance and theoretical expertise that would be sufficient to throw off balance beforehand all the inane psychoanalyses of an autobiographical work that auto-hetero-analyzes itself like a grown-up, a big grown-up with whom I invite all the psychoanalysts of the world to do a *tranche*.

Here, in this passage from *Les Commencements*, which turns the question about the question upside down, it is the Freud of the *Introduction to Narcissism* whom we are dealing with. Before this work is named in German [*Zur Einführung des Narzissmus*], I am getting there, you might, would that you might read this big upsetting of the question, even before and also after the fragment that I must cut out (I am going to read without knowing how to pitch my voice: I have never read her aloud but I am also persuaded that what I should have done today, all this time, is merely read her texts to you without a single word of interruption from me). You are going to listen to her saying *là* and *ment* and awakening beyond the question, which is still "what is it?" or "what does 'that is to say' mean [*qu'est-ce à dire, c'est à dire*]?" As she awakens beyond the question—the question "what is it?" to which we will often come back—it is not only the structure of the question and of the ontological question ("What is it?") that she takes issue with; if I may say so, it is the structure and purpose of the question in general, and the place where the "Oedipus question," as she says, is lodged, domesticated, somnambulized in it. Consequence: strongly tensed toward all the agencies of filiation and genealogy though this work may be, it is neither a family romance nor an oedipal tragedy. There is indeed conjugation or conjugality between the two almost antagonistic figures of omnipotence, the unique dead-fathers in substitution and my uniquely irreplaceable living-mother, the alliance with one of the figures being betrayed for the other and *for life*, but these are figures with six hundred voices, as you will hear, and digits, numerals, and numbers, fictional idealities whose "as if" eludes psychoanalytical knowledge and its theoretical questions after having seriously exhausted them. And where it does not elude them, the "if" of the "as if" is heteroanalytical as much as autoanalytical. And neither psychoanalysis nor Freud and his own kinsfolk can escape the analytical irony, which is the very element, the laughter of all this often tender, sometimes implacable poetics, all the less so since, by a felicitous turn of history, Uncle Freud is part of the family. He never leaves, he sleeps on a couch in the waiting room, waiting to have an X-ray. Besides, the syllable *si* of this *comme si* [as if] or of this "qua*si*" is as untranslatable, with all its homophones, as the *là* [there] together with the whole symphony of her work in *si* and in *là*,[28] with its six hundred voices and its proper nouns ending in *si*, *Messie*, *Thessie*, or in *La*, *Illa*, etc. But we are not done yet, for the *si*, the *là*, and the *-ment*, which I have just announced, operate and play throughout her writing, and their very substance is wrought into it. To read her means first to take note, with each letter, of this untranslatability. Here is then the announced quotation from *Les Commencements*, while emphasizing—I should say and explain myself later—*the quote* rather than the citation:

> Then you look like my father.
> The pieces of my father, one **here** [**ici**], one **there** [**là**], one **there**.
> And it's **there**, precisely [**là** *juste*ment], that I began to think:
> We form the **figure** that represents existence exactly [*exacte*ment],
> It is the figure three,
> You, me, the knife
> Me, you, the elsewhere.
> Before I woke up, that's [*voi*là] what I was thinking:—and it was as if [*comme* **si**] this thought—it was a question—I had to cross it [**la**] in order to wake up—there was an answer in the question in an answer in the question and so on [**ainsi** *de suite*], and a door in a door in a wall in a door and the wall rose brown and beautiful into the sky,—and this made me understand that the answer being in the Oedipus question was already in the Sphinx, and that I was in Saint Georges and that it was possible that he may have been in one of the pieces of my father, but which one?
> I had to answer the question in order to wake up but the answer was a waking up and that's [**c'est ce**] what wakes me up.
> It was [**c'était**] the silly question: why do you write? Since when have you been writing? I don't write, I must write.
> I have to write because of **us**,
> Because when I know [*sais*] that I don't know, . . .

Let us remember once and for all that *sais* is also a near homophone of *C* and *c'est*, especially in Algeria, and that the knowledge of who knows [*sait*] is allied, is closely linked with the ontological or constative or apophantic proposition that says, "It is [*c'est*]," "This is that," that is to say, which claims to answer any question in its form par excellence, namely [*à savoir*], "What is it?" Do you know what it is? Do I know it? Without speaking of an *esse*, which, till then [*d'ici là*], will wait for us a few more hours.

. . . Because when I know that I don't know,
then I have to tell myself another story
And it is ours.
In this story one has to suppress all the substantives that end in
-**ment**, in order to avoid mistakes.[29]

One has to know, till then, how to reconstitute a chain, with regard to -*ment* and with regard to the *événement* [event] (and I will
try later on to show in what sense her poetics is a poetics of the
event, in truth of the *might* [puissance] of the event, of the taking-
place, of the *replacing taking place*, of the event in potentiality [*en
puissance*], of the event whose mighty power would have come, the
coming of the "might" and of the *si*, of two kinds of *si* in French,
of a *s'il se pouvait* [if it were possible] and of a *si, mais si, si, il se
peut, ausitôt dit aussitôt fait* [yes, but of course, yes, it may be, no
sooner said than done]—I'll come back to it very quickly). The
chain of the -*ment*, its very anchor is dropped, for example with
regard to what is called *Le Portrait de ma mère*, which illustrates
and distinguishes itself with a poem on the event:

> Never does Eve even tell lies [Eve, as some will know, is the first
> name of her mother, who is alive, thank God, and here present, out-
> side literature—JD].[30]
> My mother is where she is.
> She is not where she is not.
> Eve never even tells lies,
> Her tongue and truth are tied like two serpents in a ferocious mar-
> riage to anyone willing to listen.[31]

Let us leave Eve aside for the moment, her temptation and these
serpents in Genesis. Eve-never-**even-t**ells-lies [*jamais Ève-ne-ment*]
is therefore another name for her mother, not *Elle ment* [she lies],
Élément, as I was saying from my side, that is to say, the letter
that is greater than the whole and which is therefore never where
one believes it is, on her side, but *Événement* [Event]. Since "my
mother" is where she is, one should know what it is to be on her
side, on the side of my living mother, on her own side, which
tells the time in German, *Die Zeit*, that is to say, in the feminine,

whereas for Saint Georges, called "my father" this time, time is
Latin and masculine (*tempus*), the offspring from the marriage between the one and the other being neuter: *tempora*.[32] Here then is
what I will now call the uprising of the question, the revolution of
the question, the calling of the question into crisis or into question, which resembles a genesis of the work as much as the work of
a genesis. A genesis that makes genealogy, the family romance, and
the Oedipus question tremble. Here then, I let you reconstruct the
immediate context (evoking the printed proper noun, the drawing
of a flower, etc.).

> . . . the picture, the little girl, and my name underneath. I don't
> deny it. [This "I don't deny it" already points us toward the last de-
> negation (*dernier dé-reniement*), this nondenial that I still keep in re-
> serve.—JD] This little girl is sturdy, and, nevertheless, without my
> name she would have wavered on the line between those who are and
> those who are not, and in the end she would have disappeared. She
> may be what I might have been able to have been.
>
> But the question is elsewhere, it's not under her feet, it's on her
> head. It is the question of the flower, so-called, Zur Einführung des
> Narzissmus; who the hell stuck this stalk on my head? When I was
> little there were two questions, one deadly, the other planted on my
> head at the end of an extending stalk.
>
> The first question was: Who do you love best, Mummy or Daddy?
> Through this "or," death entered, and there was nothing one could
> do about it, as soon as the question was posed, I began killing or dy-
> ing. If I had loved Daddy best, I would have said I love Mummy best
> and if I had loved Mummy best and if I had loved myself best and
> if I had loved best not to love then I would answer with the second
> question in order to crush the first, it was: You love me/him/her [*tu
> me l'aimes*]?[33]

Having taken note of what happens here to the superimposi-
tion of questions of identity and preference, and for subjects who
"become inseparable and illegible" through overlaid inscriptions,
which "in crossing each other out embrace each other" (like El
Fath over Israel with "will win" at the end), she launches another
question, again a question of the side, a question left aside or put
aside:

Another question:

Is that me [**Est-ce que c'est** *moi*, **ça**]? That didn't reply, that didn't say anything to me.

Let's do a test: let's take some paper and draw a flower of head. *The* [la] flower [*la* in italics: as often she superimposes thus the untranslatable *la*, feminine article or adverb of place, *illac*—JD]. Here are some examples:

A leaf always
bent: **a side** that is
bulging while the **other side** is sunken. And vice versa. It has no buds. It cannot reproduce.[34]

This was, by way of example, just one of these underwater excursions from one book to the other, which I would not be able to multiply, as one ought to in order to survey the shores and sides [*côtes et côtés*], all the sides of every question. And in order to show how, as Kant would say, she "orients herself in thought." In "*Was heisst: Sich im Denken orientieren?*" you know how Kant opens his reflection on rational belief (*Vernunftglaube*) and on the assent of belief in what is held to be true (*Fürwahrhalten*), in particular about the existence of God, where it depends on an "if." In her own way, as we will see, she will also demonstrate God's existence. As for Kant, in this context dealing therefore with a rational faith in God's existence, he begins by recalling what the proper meaning of the word *to orient oneself* (*sich orientieren heisst in der eigentlichen Bedeutung des Worts:* . . .) is, namely (*das heisst,* that is to say, in other words, this is called), well, the irreducible reference to the body proper and to feeling (*Gefühl*), right on my own subject (*an meinem eigenen Subjekt*) of the difference between the left hand and the right hand—of which he recalls elsewhere, in the argument of the noninterchangeability or the irreversibility of gloves, that even when there is no conceptual difference in the analysis of hands, left and right are not superposable in sensible intuition—and in the use of gloves. One side will never be superposable on the other.

The irreversible, here, is life for her, the side of life, and she orients herself in relation to life, as one says to orient oneself with a compass or by the sun.

I come back to the question of the side: down her way, on the side of what, without putting anything aside, without putting anything on the side, she bets on the side. It seems at first that for her, and I do mean for her, there is only one side and not two, and this side is that of life. Death, which she knows and understands as well as anyone, is never denied, certainly; it haunts and blows everything away, you could verify it with every word, but it is not a side, it is a nonside. This is why I—and this is probably more than a difference, a big disagreement [*différend*] between us, of which I may speak again later—I, who always feel turned toward death, I am not on her side, while she would like to turn everything and to make it come round to the side of life. For lack of time, I have to give up doing what I first wanted to do: analyzing in two books only, at both ends of the chain, from the first to the last volume to date (*Le Prénom de Dieu* and *OR*), the whole lexicon of *vivre* (insofar as it names the side with only one side, a side without another side) and all the logical, grammatical, or semantic modalities, all the variations in tone and the rules of composition, the places and subject of enunciation with which this vocabulary of living according to the side, if not of living by the side, plays. To give you a telegraphic idea of this corpus and of what I have to give up, note that *OR*, for example, opens thus: " . . . he has already given me life six times. But this could just as well have been sixty times. I don't know the date of the last one" (once again *si*, six, sixty, six hundred, and the last one), and closes with: "Life is detachment"; and in between you will have read so many times, for example, the words *vivant* [living], *vivre* [to live], *survivre* [to survive], *vif* [lively], *vives* [(a)live], and "nothing is dead," "and six hundred that's one life at least" (six hundred letters this time), and *vivre fait livre* [living makes the book], and "a dead man has just lived. A dead man still arrives/manages. To live," and: "life that is to say so little," and "everything survives us," and "I live," and "I am the place of revival," and "my life permit," and "is this called living . . . ," and "life, I don't hold you back," and "the flesh eaten alive,"

and "to live one dies," and "beat death with life," and "he chooses
to meet death alive" and "to whoever may live," and "because of
living," and "I will live alive and I will die alive. . . . Half and half
never" (which already recalls or suggests, I'll come back to this,
that life is whole and does not have two sides, it has and is only
one side, on one side only—but it is the dead father who speaks
and says here: "I will live alive and I will die alive"), and she has
just said, in italics: "*I hear everything he does not say, I think*," and
"*an egg of life*," and "*all the time I have left to live*," and "*all that we
have silenced* [avons tu] *to live and not to kill* [tuer]," and "*to live
like a shadow*," and "*to live on nothing*," and, from life to town [*de
la vie à la ville*], this extraordinary sentence, which would merit a
whole *décade*:

> It will take another hundred years before six I mount life by sheer
> strength of mind, I have the ability of a world a day with all its inhab-
> itants, a town at each station.

So, she mounts life, then, as one mounts a play but also as one
hoists sail when one resuscitates or raises a dead man. Lazarus,
arise. It is her. That is her side. Side, which is to say what?

Giving up my project, I will only take *three* typical examples of
her side, very quickly, among so many other occurrences.

There is *first* the passage already quoted from *Jours de l'an*
(1990). According to this work of fiction, for it is a work of fiction,
she calls herself the daughter of the dead fathers, but she is not on
their side, whereas she is, like "me," in the first person, "on the
side of" her living mother (singular possessive pronoun: "on the
side of *my* living mother," she says—and *living* life [*vie* vivante]
can only say in a sense, as we will see, *me*, she is always "mine," on
the side of what always signifies me, to me, mine. Moreover, it is
paradoxically because of this unilateral mine-ness that she is open
to the undecidability and to the difference of mighty powers—just
as homophony or homonymy is to be found, paradoxically, on
the side of irreducible difference, of the heterogeneous and the
untranslatable: homo- and unilaterality are more than ever prey to
the other and to difference, they are their very test and we will be

put to the test. This probably does not mean she is or feels closer
to her mother than to the dead fathers. Indeed, when one is *on
the side of,* one is not close; one has to be on the other side, on the
other side of the other, in order to be close. When one is on the
same side, paradoxically, one is not close, there is no longer any
distance or proximity; neither speed nor slowness. Nor does this
mean she takes sides with her mother against the dead fathers; as
we will see, the side she takes, like the side Joyce takes, would be
rather that of her father, but she is on the side of the living mother,
of *her* living mother, "of my living mother," whatever that may
signify.

    What can this possibly mean? That is to say what? In order to
ask this question the right way, in her/its place, let us never forget
we are also speaking of literature and fiction, even if, as I noted
above, the fiction here is hyperrealist. The one who says "I/me,"
"*I* am on the side of my living mother," while the other character,
"the author," is "the daughter of the dead fathers"—the former,
therefore, is neither the entire subject of the book, the "me" of the
book of which she is not the author anyway, since the author is a
character, nor certainly at one with Hélène Cixous here present,
right beside me, on this side, on the side and at the side of her
living mother. It is not her, but it is not another either, the one
who tells, I do not remember where, that one of the first aston-
ishments of her life, which no one has ever managed to cure her
of, at school, dates back to the day when she read "I is another."
A proposition she has never ceased to put back to work, yes, to
work, on all sides. For if she, who is here present (supposing we
know what "here present" means), is not the "I" who says "*I*, as
opposed to the author, am on the side of my living mother," she
is not simply another either. She is, let's say, beside herself, on her
own side but sitting, like another, sitting beside herself. Like her
father, as you will hear, who after his death came to sit *beside her.*
And in moving from this place, which is at once untenable and irreplaceable, she teaches us to worry about the essence of literature,
of fiction, of the institution thus named and about everything one
calls identity. As long as one has not read the side of the side of

what, on her side, she writes, one will not have approached these questions.

The *second example* of this strange *side*, at the beginning of *OR* (1997, therefore seven years later), we'll come back to that again in a moment, is a scene of quasi-resurrection. It is about bringing back to life someone whose "ghost" one catches "by a wisp [*mèche*] of life."[35] Within a limited period of time, she says, eight to fifteen days, it is possible to make life come back to life; and here again, she says, for life, "to this side": "During these days," she says, "it is still possible to bring them back to this side." The side, once again, her side is indeed the side of life (on the side of my living mother, she said, and here to bring back the dead to this side, etc.). But we will see confirmation that this side, as the side of life, has the particularity of being the only side. There is no other side than this side, the side of life. There is only one side in her geography, her geophysics, and her geology; there is only one rib [*côte*] in the body, one shore on which to fix [*une côte où river*] the departing and arriving [*arrivée*] of what happens on earth/land, and it is life—life, whence everything derives and detaches itself and toward which everything comes and comes back. Life has no other, it has no other side; and all the sides, all the asides, all the sidesteppings leave their traces on the same side of the same vein.

Finally, as a *third example* (but one could find so many others), we return to the end of *OR*, to a certain passage (I would like to find another word than these hackneyed, tired, and tiring words "passage," "page," or "sequence" to designate the fragmented units, the "quotes" that I will unfortunately have to cut out in this way. Each of these is a flow or period, a musical movement at once liquid, submarine, aerial, and yet solid, in the ether or in the sea, like a braid of unalterable threads and lines, here a weaving of voices that seek their own style and fortune in a gold mine, and which, precisely, as is said, while singing, dig and dig, searching for sparks of gleaming gold, letters, always, and which these six hundred voices find even when they do not find them). The string of lines I am going to cut out would merit centuries of reading, and I will return to this place later when I speak of the impossible, namely of the letter that does not manage to arrive [*n'arrive pas à arriver*], and of an impossible that is no longer the opposite of the possible, of might, of an impossible that is no longer on the other side of the possible. At the bottom of this underwater mine, which I scan, skim over, and satellize at full tilt, a first probe yields the following reading: "One had to be quick."[36] This "one had to be quick" follows an allusion to a certain "absolute letter." A voice says: "I imagined this letter. One had to be quick. It would say:" (colon, a blank of several lines and a new indented paragraph, which allows one to suppose, but this is by no means certain, that what follows is what this absolute letter, with which "one had to be quick," would say. Now I note, in this supposed quotation, even before reaching the shores [*côtes*] of two "asides [*à côtés*]," at least twice the word I am interested in, the word *puissant* [mighty]—as much for the spirit as for the letter of the letter. Here is the page from which I note, then, and single out and underline as well the words *puissant*, *vivre* [to live], *vie* [life], and *côté* [side]):

> One had to be quick. It would say:
> . . . the letter does not follow.
> The letter **did not come**. One year I remain willing.
> The second year I came back into this life [**vie-ci**]. I re-entered the nearby present without belief. But I never gave up on the letter. It remains **around there** [**par là**]. [Not around here (*par ici*), this time, but around there.—JD]
> **Mighty** are the places it haunts: they never fall straight into oblivion.
> **Mighty** the spirit of the letter.

You do understand that if there are "letters of omnipotence," as was said four pages earlier in a sequence awaiting us, what is said to be "mighty" here in this passage is not literally the letter, but "the places it haunts," once, and "the spirit of the letter," another time. Might is therefore granted and allied to the spirit of the letter, to spirit in the sense of specter and revenant. Of the specter that has to be "respectered" [*respectrer*], as is said elsewhere. The letter is mighty not in its arrival or its coming but in its coming back and its haunting places. Here is what follows:

> It sometimes happens that, when one abandons a house, just before the last hour, the wreck yields desperate treasures. We were house-wrecked several times. Nothing came out.
>
> At the blow my mother had emptied and replaced herself. [Remember this housewreck, you will see that Jonah and the whale have never stopped floating underwater there, like submarines, waiting patiently from one end of the work to the other, for thirty-five years.—JD]

"At the blow my mother had emptied and replaced herself." So the mother too is subject to replacement, but she is not replaced, she is not replaceable, she replaces *herself,* she had replaced *herself,* and that is how she remains a living mother: "She had emptied and replaced herself"—like every unique living being, she replaces herself without being replaced nor replaceable, without letting herself or making herself be replaced. She substitutes and metonymizes herself, but without ever being subject herself to substitution and to metonymy.

> The dead man leaves her. She never makes us **live** looking backward. Move on, move on, life is not the past.

Here, that is to say where the living mother speaks and gives orders, she is on the side of life, detached like a rib [*côte*] from the dead man who leaves her, turned toward [*du côté de*] life: "Move on, move on, life is not the past." It is indeed her mother, the mother, who orients everything; she thinks on the side of the irreversible. And she, not the author but she, the one who says "me" on the first day of the year, she is, she insists on being and saying that she is on the side of her living mother.

> All the rest goes to the children. Each their own. They live for decades with this slight thirst whose fever seizes those amputated of a message. They live on this thirst, this slight amputation. Each **on their own side** rummages through the drawers of the earth.
>
> Until the day when . . .

"Until the day when . . . " Here is the absolute exception that
we will keep coming back to, until the day when one day, once
upon a time, only once, on this date, there was the dead father,
on whose side she does not find herself, not as she finds herself on
the side of her living mother; here he comes, the dead father, one
fine day, and sits *beside her.* The phrase "to sit beside" is a phrase
that, moreover, as I can testify, she uses in life, as in literature, in
a very singular way, which has always, as ever, surprised me; but
let's move on, I will not insist, or I will risk seeming to be doing
my best to ensure that henceforth no one else could ever dare to sit
beside her, even if only for a drink:

> Until the day when in a flash I decipher my father's message: it is
> this absence of a letter that takes the place of the letter. I give you the
> page and the necessity. He **comes out** of his **deathly** apartment, he
> comes and sits **beside me** and we thus communicate through the long
> attunements of the blood. He knows that I know what he thinks.

It is always "know," isn't it [*c'est le "sais," n'est-ce pas*]. "He knows
that I know . . . " He, that's him, the one who knows that I know
what it is that I know. The secret. Then these other lines, which I
will reread otherwise later:

> At times I lend my voice to his thought and I can see that he is
> pleased. The keys are in your drawer [Your drawer: to whom is she
> speaking? Who speaks to her through the voice of her father?—JD]. I
> write to you. Yes of course I say, I am/follow your letter. I am/follow
> myself your letter to me I say [*Je suis moi-même ta lettre à moi dis-je*].

One does not know who pronounces this last sentence, he or
she, who quotes him or takes his words in her; it is pronounced in
a single breath without punctuation. I repeat it and leave it to its
reserve straightaway:

> I write to you. Yes of course I say, I am/follow your letter. I am/fol-
> low myself your letter to me I say.

One will never know who says "I," and "I say," twice. Or who
holds the pen of this *more-I* [plus-je]. This comes after the father's

deciphered message, that is to say: the absence of the letter takes the place of the letter.

I will not impose on you a statistics of all her ribs/shores [*côtes*] and sides [*côtés*]; that would take a lifetime. Just to give you an idea, in just one book, *Jours de l'an* once again, and over five pages only, here are at least four occurrences that are radically different in their meaning, function, geometry, geography, geophysiology, architecture, and limitrophy. You have all the sides, the absolute polyhedron of all the sides of the word "side," the polyphonic chiliogon or polygon of all the sides and all the shores of the earth. If I wanted to play without playing on the word *gône* [-gon], with the omega and the omicron of the syllable "gon," I would say that this poetic chiliogony of all the sides is also a georgic as theogony, a genealogy of all the divine filiations. For if *gôn* signifies the angle or the side, *gonè* is generation and *goneus*, the father in the singular, is also the father *and* the mother, the mother-father in the plural.

I enumerate merely four sides on five pages of this polygony by emphasizing with my voice without adding a word. You will hear successively the joyful movements in "side" in the next room [*à côté*], followed by "on the other side/hand [*de l'autre côté*]," then by "(a step) not on this side [*un pas de ce côté*]," and finally "from one side to the other," always between father and mother, the mother [*mère*] and the sea [*mer*]:

I.

I go there, all dead, all dead. Into the **next** room [**à côté**] so far so far from my heart. And I enter.

A blank or silence of two lines. And the voice resumes:

I, too, have forgotten a child in the **next** room [**à côté**]. When I remembered, ten years later, my mother no longer knew where the tomb was buried. This can happen to us.

But what is peculiar to the author's baby is that, once forgotten, it will come back to her mind in the end.

In the next room, then, the tomb that cannot be found, the

tomb that is itself buried, encrypted. You will have to read what follows without me; it is in *Jours de l'an*.[37]

2. The following page is still about birth, but another one, her own, this time, and about a birth before her birth, her first name before her first name, her first name before her birth:

I will continue to paint this woman's portrait.[38]

This woman will be a mother, again, the mother of all women poets who, as she says, entered into her, Clarice Lispector, Marina Tsvetayeva, closer here, but so many others too, starting with herself on the side of her own living mother.

> Everything begins to happen to her inside her mother's breast before her birth. During **that** time [-*là*] her mother speaks to her in German, and she calls her Alexander. Her mother was expecting an Alex/*ander* [a slash between Alex and the other, *ander*—JD]. The other. The spark [*éclat*] of this prenatality stays with Marina.

Éclat; I suppose at once the aura, the radiant breath but also the scandal, the sparks that fly [*coup d'éclat*], and also the shine [*éclat*] of metal, the sparkle of gold before birth, that is to say, to say it differently, the spark [*éclat*] of genius.

> The spark of this prenatality. . . . To have been what she was not. To have him. And then she was not him. It is this story of the unexpected [*d'inattendue*: feminine—JD]. We expect Alexander. And she is: the other. So it will be: her: him: *ander*: he **on the other side. The other side of her**.[39]

3. Two or three pages further, *I quote*:

> Alexander's book merely has a head start. And she, always ahead, ahead by a life, by a birth, by a separation, since she has already read, lived, lost, enjoyed everything, **on the one hand [d'un côté]** already written, already dead, but on the other [*côté*—JD] not at all, on the other not yet, on the other, woman, lover, greedy, not yet knowing anything of what she already knows. . . . **It is life itself**. Instantly the unknown will cease, and it will be death. . . . Nothing stops love. . . . We see her go toward love, in that direction, is it a wolf? is it a tree? as one goes toward the sea, in long intrepid strides [*pas*], loving ahead without knowing if the sea will be there [the sea, *la mer*, three

letters and without the *e* of *mère*—JD], but there she goes. The sea is not there. **Not on this side [pas de ce côté]**. "I was sure you wouldn't be there!" she cries.[40]

I quote still on the same page the movement of a few lines that seem to me to say something decisive about her sides of life death, and what within her comes ahead from this side, a long time ahead:

> It aims at, it touches the very belly of, women, seeking the women promised by Pushkin, announced by Rimbaud, the women up ahead. The sugar of life. But unfortunately in that time there were even fewer women than poets. It does not matter.
>
> Just because no one is there yet does not mean we should not love. She loves the women
> from after her death.[41]

4. Finally, but this is not a quadrangle, on the next page:

> She is awakened on May 3, 1926.

Here the French has *may*, with a *y*, *m-a-y*, what does that mean? That is to say what, in other words, among other things? I say "among other things and for example" because I do not know, probably, I know so little and I can only surmise, I presume that her entire text is encrypted right through, riddled with hidden references and dates, those of the anniversaries of her father's death and birth, for example: the month of May is inscribed everywhere in her corpus. *May* may be a first name: if not the first name of God, at least that of a feminine divinity, a female first name of God or of the Goddess [*D.S.*].[42] But *may*, with a *y*, may also sign, potentially [*en puissance*], the mighty power of the "might" [*la puissance du "puisse"*], "*may*," which awaits us. In a moment I will propose to derive might not from power and the possible but rather from the subjunctive "might [*puisse*]." At this provisional, unexpected stage, I would feel tempted, about this "*may*," to speak in English only and to derive everything from "*may*" and "*might*": *might this happen*; would that this might happen, oh! if [*si*] only this could happen, yes [*si*], let this happen, *might this one arrive, might this letter arrive*, might such and such happen; and the English noun *might* is also a certain power [*puissance*]. So we have in the English "*might*" at once the form *might* [le puisse] and *might* as *power* [la puissance], the verb and the noun, the optative subjunctive and the magic of the power to make or let happen. Then, besides the alliance of power, of might [*puissance*] and of the "might [*puisse*]," you have the precious alloy of desire or wish and of the granted authorization ("*might I, you may*, yes, *you might*"), of freedom or of the given grace or pardon. And since I take the liberty of connecting this to the inscription of a date ("She is awakened on May 3, 1926"), I recall that one would have to write ten theses on the dates, the play and the question of dates in *this* work—which, as we say in French, *fait date*, that is, marks an epoch, as one calls [fait] a telephone number, as we will see—and she *calls up* a name [fait *un nom*], as we will hear, as one *calls* a telephone number.

> She is awakened on May 3, 1926. This thing approaching through the distances, coming from Val-Mont through Glion sur Territet (Vaud) Switzerland, which is going to touch her in a moment, at that very hour in may . . . [43]

May again with a *y* in the French; and this time it is the hour, at that hour in *may*, and not the day in *may*; now [*or*] as regards the hour and the word *hour*, which the conjunction *or* comes from, and *encore, hanc horam*, one would have to dedicate yet another ten theses to this work of a goldsmith or watchmaker, which is literally obsessed with everything that happens to the hour [*arrive à l'heure*], happens to the signifier *heure* or *or*, and which arrives or does not arrive on time [*à l'heure*]—as well as on the spot, in a moment [*sur l'heure, tout à l'heure*].

> . . . which is soon going to touch her, at that very hour in may, is Rilke. His name in person. And his full address. [Keep this address in mind, we would never be done with it.—JD] Touch her with flapping wings, through the very distances [therefore it is not just a question of touching her from a distance at infinite speed, but of touching through the very distance, through the spacing of separation: the speed of this absolute caress is separation, the tact of a separation that

touches—JD], *mit fernen, mit Flügelschlägen,* with flapping *f* 's [*coups de f.*]. [These *coups de f.* arc not *coups de feu* (gunshots) but the flappings of these words in *f* 's that tell of the distance of the bird's flight, the flapping wing (*coup d'aile*) and its homonym in French, *elle; mit fernen, mit* **F***lügelschlägen*: telephone calls (*coups de fil*) that flit and flutter (*frôlent ou effleurent*) without touching, or barely; we will speak later of the fleeting touch (*frôlement*) of eternity.—JD] At thirty-four years old, barely awake, still fluttering **from one side to the other**, on the edge, of night, of waking, it is on this edge, in the troubled blue of the sky, that it comes toward her, the thing that is Rilke, still living and already fluttering **from one side to the other**, on the edge.[44]

Twice you have heard "from one side to the other," and each time this means two things, twice the edge on the edge of another meaning. The side is certainly an edge, it is "on the edge," but "from one side to the other" can mean the oscillation between the two edges, the two sides, as much as from the side of the other, only from one side of the other, only from a single side or only from the side of the other. Moreover, if one side seems to draw the line of an edge, the word "side," in its prevalent use, designates yet something other than a line or an edge, namely the geometry of objective figures, chiliogons, triangles, and quadrangles: the laterality or the littorality of anything whatsoever. On the side of the side where we say, on the contrary, on the side of somebody and not of something, on your side, on my side, and so on, "side" implies, with the taking of sides, the irreversible orientation of a body, an *around here* [par ici] and *around there* [par là-bas], a *here* and *there,* the subjective difference between left and right, the orientation of a body that opens the world from an absolute origin, the world as the here below [*l'ici-bas*] of an earth, a kind of topogeology or topogeorgic in which a body has sides that are also ribs, a left and a right one, a front and a back. Before behind [*devant derrière*]. And generally in this georgic, the sides come in twos (one side or the other), which is not the case in objective geometry, where so many figures, with the exception of the circle or the Moebius strip, which only have one, have more than two sides or two angles.

But if, as I suggest, life has no other side, if there is only one side, the one of living life, then the latter remains undecidable, certainly, since one does not have to decide and can no longer decide between two opposable edges or sides, but this undecidable is the place of decision which, however serious it may be, can only be *for life*. Because it is undecidable, one can decide and settle only for life. But life, which is undecidable, is also, in its very finitude, infinite. What has only one side—a single edge without an opposite edge—is in-finite. Finite because it has an edge on one side, but infinite because it has no opposable edge.

I promised not to speak of myself, of/on my side, unless as a pretext to speak of her, from her, and of/on her side, of what she sees and understands on her side by "side." I will keep my promise, for if I recall now what she said about me in this very place a few years ago, in 1992, it is not because it was about me. It will be in order to reinterpret, from the side of the side, what *she* might have meant then. She said, from the first sentence, that she had seen me at once, from the first day, walking along a crest, then on a peak.[45] At the moment I had not reflected on the reason why this strange remark had made me feel dizzy straightaway. I first said to myself, without giving it much thought: you feel dizzy because she places you too high. She exalts you and you protest, you are afraid. You do not like to be placed too high because then, it must be known, nothing but a fall or death can happen. She frightens you or she is playing at frightening you. Today I understand better why I felt dizzy, after having begun (very recently, last May) to analyze all the sides of the side in her work. Your head spins, I then said to myself, in the first place because when you find yourself walking along a crest, you simply no longer have a side. It is as if, in order to place me too high, at the highest, on the summit of a hill [*côte*], she had simply, in raising [*élevant*] me thus, taken away [*enlevé*] my side, all the sides, not taken out a rib [*côte*] in order to procreate her mother Event, but, in getting to the very last extremities, she had simply taken away all the sides of me, all my sides being then removed from all sides. No more edge [*bord*] for me. No more death, maybe, since life has no opposite edge, but no more edge at all, on no side, more exposed than ever at/to the height to which I thus saw myself raised, doomed not to put a foot wrong or step to one side [*pas de côté*] once, without the slightest safeguard, closer than ever to the fall or the unforgivable mistake. So I would have no side at all, no side for sidestepping [*pas de côté pour un pas de côté*]. That's why now I do not know where to put myself. At the slightest step aside I fall, I lose, and if it is not on one nonside of the abyss, it is on the other. I'd just better stay put [*je n'ai qu'à bien me tenir*]. I understand better now why, despite the grace I was thus given, I felt like walking back down to the valley without delay like a child, dreaming of only one thing: to dream after having been tucked in on both sides [*border*].

I have another reason to evoke this strange scene—a "me" without a side in short, without sidestepping and without a stitch in the side [*sans pas de côté et sans point de côté*], for let us never forget the stitch in the side and the breathlessness, and that the side and the rib always protect the heart, the chest, and above all the lungs against mortal threats, for example tuberculosis, which Georges died of—who besides was himself also defined as *A Climber* (this is the title of a whole sequence in *OR*: "a climber" who climbed the peaks of Davos like a hero, from summit to summit, when she has just said "I go from father to father."[46] There is one of these fathers who resembles her father and of whom she says that he is a "climber devoted to the Crests [*Crêtes*]"—this time *Crêtes* is spelled with a capital, like the famous chemin des Crêtes in Algiers). But as everyone knows, I am not her father. Besides, each time I read her allusions to crests, to peaks, to the summit, to the climber (her father, her dead-fathers), I think of the great tradition, the filiation, the ancestral ascension of Mont Ventoux, the scene of forgiveness and conversion, and of Petrarch's *secretum meum*.[47]

In *Jours de l'an*, the scene with Hokusai and Rembrandt about the truth to paint and the dream of painting Fujiyama, one sentence tells of the assault on hills and ribs [*côtes*]: "And since he got along well with them (death, the mountain), having lived with them for ninety years, that's what happened" (that is to say, "to conquer Fujiyama in painting" and thus attain Truth).[48] As for the side or the rib under which the heart beats and the threatened lung breathes, what she cites from her father's medical thesis begins with these words, between *border* [to line] and *broder* [to embroider]:

> I can see in the right costo-clavicular angle a finely **lined** [**bordée**] cavity the size of a finely **embroidered** [**brodée**] apple in the midst of a diseased parenchyma . . . [49]

One should always protect this vulnerable *heart* and lungs under the ribs, put them in the shelter of an armor and of a *cotte de mailles*, spelled c-o-t-t-e—and you will find more than one *cotte de mailles* in her work. *Cotte de mailles* is called "coat of mail" in English. For example in *Les Commencements*, for the distribution of her being between father and mother, as between *here* and *there*, untranslatably beside Here [*à côté d'Ici*] and beside There [*à côté de Là*], she summons and conjures up the appearance of the sides beside the coat [*cotte*] in a passage from which I can cut out only a few lines but which would be made to intersect with the entire work, starting with *La*, the book that bears the title *La*, if we had the time:

> . . . of a woman and a male of another species, in accordance with what I look like. In any case I **take** after [**tiens** *de*] my father, and I am **held** by [**tenue** *par*] my mother. In general, when I am under my own eyes, or under those of Saint Georges when he clasps me in the red coat [**cotte**] of mail, and tells me that my name is You, I feel that I am a high, shining object, made of one piece, everything is far all of a sudden and so violently that the problem of **Here or There** poses itself right between my eyes, clashes head-on with me, makes my oldest tears flow, makes my nose into the axis **of both sides, beside-Here** and **beside-There**, almost splits me . . . [50]

About the high idiomatic content [*teneur*] or standard [*tenue*] of this genealogical diagnosis, which hinges [*tient*] on two moods of *tenir* (active or middle voice, more or less transitive and passive intransitive: I *take after* [tiens de] my father, I am *held by* [tenue par] my mother, where the word *tenir* is merely the untranslatable homonym, the double of itself that takes place only once in

France), one would obviously have to read the ten thousand pages that come before or after, notably about the letter *H*, which here puts into play *Ici* with *Here* and *Hier* but elsewhere, for example in *Jours de l'an*,[51] will gather all the *haches* [aitches and hatchets].[52] The hatchet is cast like a letter:

> She had cast him a letter. Alas, it is the one that does not arrive . . . . There is the hatchet [*hache*]. The hour. The story begins before us. . . . Each time the letter does not arrive, Tristan turns to the wall and I weep. I do not want this. The hour—the wall—the hatchet.

Or else:

> And the title that Balzac did not give his narrative is: *Do not touch the hatchet.* Because in the end he did not know anymore who the hatchet was. [The hatchet would be somebody here.—JD] We begin telling a story so as to return a blow, but in the end, while we have been writing, the hatchet has turned.[53]

The hatchet turns like the hour, the zero hour [*l'heure H*], and like history, with a small or capital *h*, more or less silent, this letter comes back to strike its origin, this "hatchet that must not be touched," "the hatchet is mad, it kills whoever touches it." The letter *H*, to initial the monogram of her name, to cut between her first name and her patronymic name, comes back everywhere, and everywhere back to itself, and each time one cites her, one would have to say, as always, *et passim* (which would allow us to add in passing a *si* to the list: *possim*, that I might, *et passim*). I will never say enough about this hatchet in order to honor the first part of my title, to which I will come back when I begin, for I have not begun yet. With her, one always has to begin and begin again and, as I have already said, I will merely multiply the palinodes of rebeginnings on the threshold.

Yes, before I forget, I have another reason for citing this scene of a "me without any side" and for treating it as a literary event, if you wish, like a scene staged at Cerisy, since it is in this very place that I saw myself, suddenly saw myself walking on the summit, along a crest without edge, without any other side than the vertiginous law calling upon me, in short, to hold myself erect between two abysses. There is indeed another reason, which I do not know what to do with, short of intensifying in the dark the formalization of this strange logic of the edge without an opposite edge, a unique side on the one hand [*d'un côté unique*], certainly, but not without another, quite the contrary. For the unique side is certainly the side that is dissymetrically turned toward the other, oriented, exposed, or held to the other. But precisely this remains a unique side without another side, and this would be life itself (remember what we said a moment ago: this unique side, this uni-laterality is *of life for life*, life itself, life promised to life, sworn life, whereas death, which she knows and understands as well as anyone, is not denied, certainly, but it is not a side, it is a nonside). Well, in the formalization of this strange topogeology that is her own, which is neither merely coastal nor simply littoral or lateral, maybe one should also, I would not say integrate, for this is what by definition cannot be integrated, but inscribe the uninscribable catastrophe, namely the possibility of a side first without other, certainly, but also without (a) me [*sans moi*]: not a me without any side along a crest, but the side without other and without (a) me.

The possibility of this absolute catastrophe is at once evoked and warded off at the end of *Beethoven à jamais ou l'existence de Dieu* (1993) in the next to last episode of the last chapter (chapter 9, ten minus one), entitled "The Betrayal." This is where the phantasm, if one may say so, of a betrayal betrays her. This also happens in a château, a bit like here. Of this betrayal, she ends up saying that she complains about it less than she confesses: for it is first of all her own ("This, she says, is not a complaint. It is a confession: I very nearly betrayed my love. . . . I very nearly died"). The signature of a grace or pardon [*grâce*], which pardons [*gracie*] in corresponding to the title of the Overture, namely (it is thus the title of the "Overture"): "Overture. To know that I am going to die." Three graces, at the end of *Beethoven*, three times the word (of) grace or pardon [*mot de grâce*], the grace that pardons [*la grâce qui gracie*] ("infinite grace," "minimal grace," "small grace"),[54] but

a grace of "whoever always grants everything and for ever."⁵⁵ For
ever, that is to say, isn't it, "for life": grace grants life for life.

Of this Beethovenian finale, which I will let you hear and listen
to on your own, of these pages beautiful as madness, madly sublime and painful, of this hymn to faith when it wins over suicide
and the death drive, I merely want to note here that it describes
the worst moment of betrayal in the passage toward another side,
a wholly other side this time, different from all the others, because
it is a "*side without other, without (a) me.*" I read, I try to read:

> How quickly she lost her life: it was a shock of terror. Thus one can
> pass—from one second to the next—**to the other side**—**to the hor-**
> **rible other side**—**the side without other, without (a) me.**⁵⁶

A betrayal worse than death, but the death of a body that she
was able, this time, to catch in order to bring it back to this side.
You will note that the worst trial thus described also contained,
without the slightest contradiction with this monstrous other side
of the side without other and without a me, an experience of the
side-by-side, of a pseudo-proximity worse than all the separations,
worse than betrayal itself and absolute perjury. Under the subtitle "Author," here again, would that you might read this as well,
which also tells of a first and only time:

> For the first time in her life she saw him from the outside [*du de-*
> *hors*]. Beside himself [*hors de lui*]. Outside to outside [*dehors à de-*
> *hors*].
> They play the last symphony. [It is Beethoven, isn't it, in this châ-
> teau.—JD] The hall is full of abyss. Closely separated. Side by side in
> a proximity as irreparable as an amputation. "I have loved a scythe,"
> she thought. [This time it is not a hatchet but a scythe.—JD]
> Side by side. Nothing happened. Not the slightest trace of already-
> encounter or of recognition.⁵⁷

A little later, a few pages further, in a notebook, she writes, then
citing this notebook, "**beside** the false notes . . . the somewhat
coded messages," or "The rest of her climbs up **the rib** [*grimpe* **la**
côte] inside a body almost entirely in ruins."

This is almost the end of another immense book, the only one in which, to my knowledge, and right from the first page, the word *Side* is written with a capital, like the name of God, in short, since the book bears the subtitle *or the existence of God: Beethoven à jamais ou l'existence de Dieu.* On the first line of the book, right from the first words, comes what follows:

> We live in the middle of life [the first lines of Dante's *Inferno*, I sup-pose, haunt this incipit of *Beethoven,* which nearly ended with the hell of betrayal: "Midway life's journey, *Nel mezzo del cammin di nostra vita mi ritrovai per una selva oscura*"—JD], **the sides of the middle**, one never sees them, it is better not to see them. Thus life seems to us without end and thus this is how it is so [without end and without a side—JD]. As long as the flight lasts.
>
> **On the sides of the middle** stands the God. What He sees from the side, it is better never to manage to see it.
>
> It sometimes happens that a violent gust of wind blows us away **to the side of the Side**. [Capital, for the one and only time, to my knowledge: there would thus be in her work only one Side with a capital, only one occurrence of this unique Side, and it would be the name, the first name or the surname (*surnom*) of God: the Side.—JD] Better not look, better close your eyes. Once I saw, I almost saw, I nearly saw the scene from our God's point of view, all I know is that it was deadly, to see oneself, to see ourselves, us the human creatures living in time, I nearly understood death, life, . . .

I suppose—it is a hypothesis—that this deadly moment on the Side (capital) of God, this violent gust of wind that blows us away to the side of the Side, the one of God or death, this mo-ment of the "I nearly [*j'ai failli*]" ("I nearly understood death, life . . . "—both at the same time), announces the end, the end of life and the end of the book, the "I nearly" failed [*"j'ai failli" faillir*], the "he nearly failed," the necessity or fatality of "he failed or he nearly failed" of the betrayal ("to the other side—to the horrible other side—the side without other, without [a] me." "This is not a complaint. It is a confession: I very nearly betrayed my love." And three lines later: "I very nearly died").

You may remember we were still prowling, navigating by sight, on the edge, in the vicinity or in sight of the shores of these *Jours de l'an* where twice "I" says "I": "I cannot look the answer in the face. . . . *I* am on the side of my living mother."

It is impossible, it will be forever impossible (this is the essence, the function, and the event of what is called literature), to decide who says "I" in the sentence "I cannot look the answer in the face," where moreover it contains indissociably the memory of the preceding question: "Your dead father, would you like it if he wasn't?" Is it Hélène Cixous, the author, or "me"? Who is it? Who knows who is what she calls "me," what she, not the author as a character in the book but the author herself, she [*lui-même, elle*], Hélène Cixous, calls "me"?[58] And I murmur around here in an aside that I often ask myself the same question, more or less the same, about her father: what would have happened, around here, happened to her and to the world, to us, around here, if Georges Cixous had not died young and died thus, a knight wounded under his coat of mail? What of her life—her work, then? Would *we* have wished for it to be otherwise? Can *we*, in front of all these works of fiction, look the answer in the face? I cannot, and this is why I close the parenthesis of this aside here and silence this murmur, a murmur that is already haunted, around here, by an unavowable parricide, which moreover is all the more impossible, and no less unthinkable than a matricide, since it would be deferred postmortem. Is there a parricide in progress, and can one think of a parricide postmortem? But is not every parricide postmortem, and posthumous, on this unique Side, that of God's existence? On page 36 of *OR*, just before "Silenced Alive [*Tues vives*]," an extraordinary address is probably addressed, without naming him, to a king, Oedipus Rex or rather Oedipus at Colonus from the point of view of the eyes and tears of Antigone before the secret of her father's tomb. The address speaks of whoever is "condemned to die posthumously," even if "no dead person has ever spoken their last word." And here again the truth of an answer cannot be looked in the face nor told face-to-face. In the previous paragraph: "I am before the truth. Pity puts her hand on my mouth and I don't scream." She cannot look in the face nor speak what she is dying with desire to shout.

Now this "I" (a personal pronoun, a person's first name [*pronom de personne, prénom de personne*], (no) more-I [*plus-je*], you might say, on account of a no-person's first name, a first name that hardly bears the name of the dead father), this personal pronoun of a (no-)person [*pronom personnel de personne*], which, however much of a pronoun it may be, replaces nobody, does not answer the question "we" are told or posed, not posed but told in fictional form: it is as if ("It is as if someone said to us: your dead father, would you like it if he wasn't?"). *I* does not answer this question that is addressed to *us*. Not only "I," an "I," a person's pronoun, do(es) not answer such a quasi-unacceptable question; he or she cannot look the answer in the face while saying "I." "I cannot look the answer in the face." Which gives one to understand that the answer to the question *we* are posed exists; and the proof of its existence is precisely that I know it well enough, terribly enough, I am terrified enough by it to know I cannot look it in the face. What is it one cannot look in the face? Nothing. The sun, as one says? The portrait of the Sun?[59] No. Nothing, maybe a "nothing mightier than everything," she says (these are the words that describe the betrayal, at the end of *Beethoven*: "It is a nothing mightier than everything").[60] No, literally, it is never something, not even the sun or death one cannot look in the face—but only sideways. It is always somebody one can or cannot look in the face. So *who*? *Who* is this answer that I cannot look in the face? Because the answer is not this or that, it is somebody. One should no longer ask: from whom does this answer come that I cannot look in the face? But: who comes instead, at the place of this answer that I cannot look in the face? Maybe that is the secret of this writing. But the thing is even more terrifying as soon as the "I" who says "I cannot look the answer in the face" is an undecidable pronoun between "the author and me," therefore between the author as the daughter of the dead-fathers and me, as me, "on the side of my living mother." "I" (the I) do(es) not know on which side I am, on which *side* the I, who is another, is, finds itself or does not find itself. I know that I do not know. I is the one who knows not to know, *I* who know that I know that I do not know. Like I. Like me. On which side.

Of death or life. Like me. Like me, she often plays, but it is not a game, deliberate or not, with the infinite memory of all the ancestors, with all the dead fathers and living mothers she conjures up, and over whom she watches as no one else can.

(I intimated that I will not speak of myself. I will not show myself face on. Only, and again, quickly in passing, from behind, as when I once gave a presentation on the thought of death. But allow me one next to last parenthesis of an exceptionally personal nature, outside of literature, or at the crossroads between literature and what one calls life, precisely on the subject of the chiasmus and the genealogical crossing or the crossroads [*croisée*]—since *croisée* is the name chosen for this *décade*. Well, I recently discovered that where for her, on her side, at least for the author, the daughter is the daughter of the dead-fathers, whereas, she says, *I* am on the side of my living mother, well I, I in life, had a father (now dead) who was called Haïm Aimé, Aimé being merely the French or Christian transliteration of Haïm, that is to say, as you know, life. My father was therefore called Life—he was called "Life" all his life, for life. Life: *aimé* [loved]. Now what was my mother called? Well, like her dead father, her father Georges, but in the feminine: my mother was called Georgette. A perfect chiasmus: my mother would be on the side of her father, so that where I am, and that is true, also on the side of my mother Georgette, for I take after her, I would be, as a result, on the side of her father Georges, of the father of her fathers, of her name of the father; and where she, the author at least, is the daughter of the dead-fathers, she would also be among others the georgic daughter of Georges-Georgette, the blind Antigone this time and therefore also to some extent my mother's daughter. As if we were potentially siblings from the two sides of families of which the least one could say is that they have no relation with each other whatsoever. Not to mention that my only uncle on my mother's side, my mother's only brother, was not called Freud, my nuncle Freud, but also Georges—like his sister Georgette, and this uncle Georges—who had a limp, was the ethical superego of the family. But as the mixture, the misalliance, or the promiscuity that I am about to hazard between the filiations is presumably not to her liking, I close the parenthesis and quietly withdraw.)

Ecce homo. No longer homophony or homonymy, but *Ecce homo.* Like "me," as a me, the one who says "I" without being able to look in the face the answer to the question that is addressed to *us* and which therefore she sees enough to know that she cannot look it in the face, like me, she, Hélène Cixous or Hélène Cixous, may be playing with the "Why I Am So Wise," at the opening of *Ecce Homo.* Nietzsche the author and Nietzsche himself are both heard here, as in one voice split into two by the chance of their existence, of their being-there (*Das Glück meines Daseins*), and underlining "maybe," this double Nietzsche names a fatality, a destiny that can only be expressed in the form of an enigma (*Rätselform*). This enigmatic destiny is that his father is dead inside him, he is his father, he bears in himself his father already dead, he says: I am "*als mein Vater bereits gestorben*": but the same "I" says: I am my mother, I live like my living mother and I live growing old like my mother, I live and I grow old, I grow old like my living mother (*als meine Mutter lebe ich noch und werde alt*). This is what I called in the past, at the time of *La logique du vivant* (Jacob's book [*The Logic of Life*]), the logic of the living woman [*la vivante*]. Nietzsche's "I" is also double, when it speaks of his "double origin (*diese doppelte Herkunft*)." "I know both, I am both (*ich kenne beides, ich bin beides*)." The father, I mean Nietzsche's father, died very young too, before the age of forty. And when he reaches the age of the father's death, I mean of Nietzsche's father, he tells us that he too became almost blind ("I lived and yet without being able to see three paces ahead").

Concerning blindness, you will find the passage I have extracted from *Jours de l'an,* on the subject of the difference between the author and me, between the daughter of the dead fathers and the one who says *I* am "on the side" of "my living mother," at the very beginning of the chapter in *Jours de l'an* (1990) entitled *Self-Portraits of a Blind Woman.* A title that, in a disturbing way, sounds like another one, that of a book published the same year, 1990, *Mémoires d'aveugle: L'autoportrait et autres ruines,*[61] which I thought I had to choose for an exhibition and its catalogue without knowing. With-out seeing [*voir*] and without knowing [*savoir*]: neither whether I was able to read and, as she would say, "forgetread [*oublire*]" straightaway what I would have read (this happens to us all the time), nor especially without seeing or knowing, which I learned only two years ago, when I read a text entitled *Savoir*, namely [*à savoir*] that she too, throughout her life, like Nietzsche, was almost blind and had not been able to see three paces ahead.[62] But this is only the first example among thousands of others of these prob-lems of identity and sight, of double life [*double vie*] and double vision [*double vue*], and of the *oublire* that follows from them. In order to prepare what follows and to prolong my epigraph—but this long lecture will be nothing but an epigraph in the form of a series of digressions, ellipses, and parentheses—I will read a few lines on the facing page. There the author lets *The Author* speak (one can see the name *The Author*, in italics, preceded by a co-lon—the author is a character, a persona of the book of which he is the author, and he speaks). I single out at least these words in order to prepare what follows:

> There is in me [says the author—JD] an unknown force that writes before me, against me, and that I dread this time more than ever. It is she who is my death.
> The solution? To write by surprise. To have jotted everything down in flashes. To telegraph. To go faster than death. And far from this book whose fields she haunts.[63]

And whose haunting fear she sings.[64] To go faster than death, she says. To telegraph. That is where I had thought I would begin, in the first stage of the preparation of this prelude: not with a post-card, nor with a letter, but with a telegram, even with a telephone call. So I thought I would begin thus (here is another possible rebeginning):

Now [*or*] toward the end of *OR*, from one page to the next, you could have *read* but without reading, very quickly and almost without seeing them, a few sentences.

These sentences, you could have read them without reading them, that is to say, seen them pass, like furtive or fugitive
shadows, maybe at a speed that is difficult to measure. You could
have . . .

When I repeat "you could have" thus, "you could have read
without reading so quickly, at a lively pace," I also mean to say
"you may have been able" to read without reading the acceleration
of these shadows between life and death. Or else "you may not
have been able . . . " But above all "I wish you might have [*eussiez-
vous pu*] . . . " And better still "would that you might have read
. . . [*puissiez-vous avoir lu . . .*]," "Oh, if [*si*] only you could have!
But yes [*si*], you could . . . "

Why thus use "power" excessively? The verb *pouvoir*, rather?
And why conjugate it thus?

"Would that you might [*puissiez-vous*] have read": I can only
say this by implying "would that you might," now, henceforth, in
the future-to-come [*à l'avenir*], have read these sentences, even if
without reading them, that is to say at once hearing and glimpsing
such sentences, which *do say well* [disent bien] (because they do
indeed [*disent bien*]) what they say, and which they say without
delay and without causing delay, at full speed, sentences that in
truth *pronounce* at once *life* [vie], *vision*, and *speed* [vitesse] to the
letter.

She says, for example, from one page to the next: "My **life** depends on my address [*je* **vis** *d'adresse*]."

Further on: "My **life** depends on (**seeing**) letters [*Je* **vis** *des
lettres*]."[65]

Further on: "The letters of **omnipotence** are naturally of a small
format. Notes at high speed [**vit***esse*]. **At the sight** [à la vue] of the
envelope, one is sa**ved** already [*sau***vé d***éjà*]."[66]

Through the grammatical modality of this subjunctive of the
optative kind, which is the strange tense of this *puisse* [might] or
puissiez-vous [would that you might] (read or read without reading), which I addressed to you like a kind of fervent or sighing
plea? Oh, if only you could read! And precisely with regard to the
vivacity of these sentences?

Yes, *life* [vie], *vision, speed* [vitesse], you hear well, from the first syllable. The first syllable is, literally, *alive with vi-* [en vie]. And life, like the *v-i* of the syllable *vie*, remains untranslatable through all these words that it initiates (*la vie, je vis, vitesse, vision, vivacité, vivement*, etc.).

In the beginning, in principle, *en arkhè*, was life, and life is kept, alive, beginning again from one word, one syllable to the next.

Vivement—and the French word *vivement* should from now on accompany all our movements, vivacious, *vivace, allegro vivace*, it would set the rhythm and the note of everything that awaits us, whether I pronounce it or not. For *vivement*, in our language, not only allies life and speed, vivacity or the lively pace as acceleration. *Vivement* says something about the desire or the optative, precisely, about the subjunctive mood and the time to come, which I was speaking of just now in relation to the "would that you might" read, etc.: look lively and read [*vivement que vous lisiez*], or oh, that the letter would arrive [*vivement que la lettre arrive*], would that it might arrive, fast [*vite*], according to acceleration itself and the absolute impatience of my desire, which would like to make it arrive straightaway, without delay, briskly [*vivement*].

Vivement que—this untranslatable phrase says at once life, the vivacity of life, the acceleration of speed, and the mighty impatience of the wish. Of the wish even before will [*vouloir*] and power [*pouvoir*], which it gives nevertheless. The wish comes before everything; it lives before everything, before knowing [*savoir*], having [*avoir*], being able [*pouvoir*], even wanting [*vouloir*]. As you are about to see [*voir*]. Literally. For you have straightaway, briskly [*vivement*], fast [*vite*], at full tilt, at high speed [*à grande vitesse*], the vision of the letter that parades before your eyes: I saw or live [*vis*], all the time, always, presently and in the past, I saw/live on letters [*je vis des lettres*], she says, I saw/live them, you saw/live, according to the homonymy, live life [*vis la vie*], that life should live [*que vive la vie*], oh, that the living of life [*vivement que* puisse *vivre le vivre de la vie*] and of visibility in all times and tenses *might* live, that life may live for life and in order to see, at full speed, briskly [*vivement*]: at all times but at a speed that, playing with time, outplays time. As if in time, in the *interval* of time, everything went so fast that there would be no time anymore. In the interval that spaces out the times and tenses, there is no more time, and this is the infinite acceleration of speed. At a glance, right now, in the twinkling of an eye even (*Augenblick*): vision, quick [*vite la vision*].

The address of which she speaks here, now, in the first appearance of *vis*, which I have just quoted ("*Je vis d'adresse*," she says), may also be, as you are about to hear, the postal or epistolary address, where she lives, down her way, the address to which the letters, the "notes at high speed," are destined. But this address is first of all her own, the address of *her* gesture. For here the word "address" describes first the deft agility of the hand and fingers, the dexterity of a play of writing with the letter, a body as light as a feather, whose incalculable, gracious calculation, even more adroit than dexterity itself [*plus adroite que l'adresse*], goes so fast that it outspeeds the letter, sometimes by removing punctuation (nobody knows better how to punctuate, in my opinion, and to punctuate is to write, nobody knows better how to remove or *spirit away* [enlever] punctuation than Hélène Cixous, yes, spirit away—whether it be marked or not, her punctuation is spirited (away) [*enlevée*]— and one should not allow oneself to speak of *OR*, as of all her other books, without first dealing with punctuation: before the letter, there is her punctuation, which is like the first silent letter of all her letters and the gear change for all her different speeds). She watches over punctuation as no one else can:

> HE KEEPS ME SEPARATE, he leaves me the state of engagement as a legacy, I inherit cellars holes stairwells and flying ladders. My life depends on my address [*Je vis d'adresse*]. To cast the word over the wind and receive the letter without fail absolutely long before it comes before my face. Straddling the interval.

She receives the letter before it arrives.

How does she do it? What is this might? That is the address. She only has to say "would that the letter *might* arrive," "oh, that it would arrive [*vivement qu'elle arrive*]," and the letter is already here, almost before the end of the sentence.

It is enough to know how to hear [*s'entendre à entendre*] *vivace* the music of *vivement* and the mighty power of this "might." Still one needs to know how to utter it. Still one needs to know how to pro-duce it and do so even when one does not utter it. The "might" may be silent, it may remain as a preverbal trace and still do what it does not utter.

As this address is her own (at once down her way and her own way of doing things, the way she really knows, with a body as light as a feather), as this address outspeeds the letter, well, the absolute speed is in some way gained a priori. It is gained on time by the letter. The address outspeeds the letter, but the letter outspeeds time, it goes faster than time, if one may say so and if one can make this impossible thing happen or arrive: to outspeed time, to go faster than speed itself, to outspeed speed, thus to overtake space and time, to pass or "double" space and time, as one says about passing a vehicle in French. I'd rather say *doubler* for two reasons. I'd rather say *doubler*, here, because, as always when I prefer anything whatsoever, it is untranslatable—and what she writes is, according to me, as I will further explain, a major and unique experience of the untranslatable; I also prefer doubling, here, because what gains *in* speed and *on* speed, time and space, gains in passing or "doubling," according to the law of the double, of the substitution of the unique for the unique, which aims for its own specter and for itself, replacing itself at its place, almost without moving. The letter, therefore, is gained as much as it gains, gained as it reaches or gains the address, as one "gains" a place, in French, when one arrives there, through a felicitous homonymy, by the grace of the untranslatable homonymy of these two addresses in France. The chance of this homonymy—(the) address is first of all an address—reveals a chance of the letter with which she plays with brilliant dexterity [*adresse*] and grace. In order to make or rather let the letter arrive "without fail absolutely long before it comes before my face," I give up listing all the occurrences of the word "address," of addresses of hers; it would be a job for life.

I have just said two things and I have said them too quickly, always too quickly. (In parenthesis: she goes faster than speed, whereas I go at once too slowly and too fast—which means that I always ask myself how we managed to meet, to read and write each other. Unless, turning this encounter between two different people as different as we were into such an improbable, unpredictable, and unbelievable chance, this difference in rhythm might be the veritable essence of this encounter: an encounter that would not be unbelievably, improbably, and miraculously unpredictable would not be an encounter. An encounter has to remain casual [*de rencontre*], improbable, risky, fortuitous, unprovable, and forever alien to knowledge. One will never know—what is called knowing—if one was able to meet somebody—what is called meeting. Against common sense, I believe that the destiny of fate [*destinée du destin*] is made of these improbable, even impossible encounters, encounters impossible to know, see or foresee, calculate, irreducible to science and consciousness, which is another way of speaking about a certain unbinding [*déliaison*], the extraordinary dissociation between the thought of fate [*destin*] or even of destiny and, on the other hand, the very idea of destination. There should not be any relation between fate and destiny on the one hand, and destination on the other hand. I close the parenthesis.) I had just said two things too quickly that have something to do with homonymy and that which arrives. First that her letter, therefore, *gains itself* as it reaches or gains the address, as one "gains" a place, in French, when one arrives there, by the grace of the untranslatable homonymy of these two addresses in France, the chance of this homonymy, the doubling [*doublure*] of the address, in the envelope of its word, being a miracle of the letter with which she plays with incomparable dexterity [*adresse*] and grace while writing or dreaming, which she does all the time at the same time. So that a letter may arrive or rather in order to leave to, give to, or take away from the letter its time (for she does all that to the letter at once: she gives the letter its time, she leaves it time, but in so doing she takes (away) its time), to make and let the letter arrive "without fail absolutely long before it comes before my face."

Two things, then, I have just said them too quickly, always too quickly: on the one hand the magical homonymy of (the) address (which is (the) address itself), on the other hand that she, the great magician of the letter, knows how to allow the letter to be made to arrive [*s'entend à laisser faire arriver la lettre*]—or what arrives in general, let us call that the event of what comes, the *arrivance* of the *arrivant*. To allow the *arrivant* to be made to arrive to the letter [*arriver . . . à la lettre*], I would like to write this in one word or in any case in several words whose syntax would be sealed with a hyphen: allow-the-*arrivant*-to-be-made-to-arrive-to-the-letter.[67]

Two things, then, a double thing.

First the homonymy—which may be a homophony but which I prefer calling *homonymy* because it will concern the name, the proper noun and not only the phonic quality of the syllable. When a phoneme becomes untranslatable, it begins to resemble a proper noun. Homonymy will also be the place of all metonymies, of all the substitutions operated by this great opus of substitution. Well, if I already insist on the homonymy, as I will again and again, it is because I would like, much later, I do not know exactly when, during the course of this session, to select this question of homonymy and therefore of untranslatability as a main thread. For homonymy is, as you know, the crux of translation; it is what, in a language, signals and signs the untranslatable. It is the cross the translator has to bear, which says: "Who goes there, halt, here thou shalt not translate me, thou shalt not be able to render the homonymy, that is to say, return the letter to its address, thou shalt not be able to translate the two addresses, the two meanings of the word *address* by a single word in thy language"; if I was given the time, I could demonstrate scientifically not only that *address* is not, far from it, the only example in this work, not only that there are many other, spectacular ones, but that the entire work of Hélène Cixous is literally, and for this reason, untranslatable, therefore not far from being unreadable, if reading still remains a kind of translating (paraphrase, circumlocution, metaphrase). Yes, I would like later, I do not know when but I hope today, to select this question of homonymy as a main thread (not only for the homonymy of all her words, but even for her very name, the homonymy between Hélène Cixous and Hélène Cixous, the double between her life and her works as well). I would like to select it as a main introductory thread, among other possibilities, with a view to analyzing the historical and political situation of this life and these works in the world, the public and private resistances that its nationalization and globalization in progress are up against. In progress, through resistance itself, by dint of accumulated denial to the point of explosion, whatever time this may take, for time, for a time that basically no longer matters. I would like to venture later a diagnosis and a prognosis in this respect. A subtitle for a report to an academy: What will globalization make of Hélène Cixous's homonyms?

The other thing I said too quickly was, I quote myself, please forgive me: "In order to make or *rather* [plutôt] let the letter arrive 'without fail absolutely long before it comes before my face.'" I emphasize *plutôt*. Why *plutôt*? And how to spell *plutôt*, the homophone of *plus tôt* [earlier]? What is it about, in other words? Well, that she might *make arrive* or, rather, that she might *let arrive*. This does not appear to be the same thing. To make arrive is not to let arrive. This appears to be a wholly other experience of the *arrivant* or of the event, doesn't it? Isn't it? To make come is not to let come, is it?

Well yes, for her, it is.

If I manage [*arrive*] to make you hear what the mighty power of this "might" is, then you will see the difference between *make come* and *let come* vanish at an infinite speed. Between what one glibly calls activity and passivity, provocation and expectation, work and passion, power and receiving, giving, taking, and receiving. And this miracle would come about in the writing of her own language, whose coming, event, and *arrivance* would lie precisely in this effectiveness, in this *coup*, which abolishes the difference between *making come* and *letting come*. The grace, the address, would lie in making while letting, in making come while letting come, in seeing come without seeing come.

Naming thus the writing of her language, I ask myself whether I am not already summoning, before her father, her mother, whose presence radiates over all of us here—and not her mother tongue, which was French, but her mother's language, which she knows like no one else, and in which, as you well know, the difference between *making come* and *letting come* remains at times indistinguishable: *kommen lassen* means at once *letting come* and *making come*, letting arrive and ordering to come.

This homonymic *address* of the letter in language (her address is an address, two addresses in one) forms a powerful tautology, an effective magic, a tautology that makes or lets happen/arrive what happens/arrives. This is everything but a formal tautology that would spend itself in reiterating the identical. This tautology engenders the event, it is even, as if the same, might itself. The mighty power to make or to let come about, graciously to accord the event with letting/making come about [*laisser faire advenir*]. The difference between letting come and making come is annulled. It is carried away to this address and by this mighty power, and annulled in the circular annulus of this extraordinary tautology: the mighty power to let/make come what comes. In an infinitely active and infinitely passive way.

What is might, then? This might? How should one hear and understand this word in the skillful address of her language? That is what I would like to take my time and explain slowly.

If I say without delaying that "vi," "v-i," whichever way you write or hear it, are the letters of an infinite word, the element of a borderless term, which has to be measured against the omnipotence of a gold digger; if I add that this gold digger who speaks (words) of gold [*parle d'or*] knows how to convince you that he would not be digging for gold if he did not know the art of the address and did not have a genius for having found it already, then you would want to see proof.

You would be right, but one must also want to hear proof, and since I know it, I will endeavor, with all the humility necessary, to comply with your request.

Now [*or*] toward the end of *OR,* as I was saying, you could read this, which *does say well* [dit bien] (I emphasize), which in truth pronounces *life, vision, speed* to the letter. I emphasized "does say well" for reasons that will become clear later; they regard the *well saying* [bien dire] as much as a certain way of blessing—benediction.

In order to see the letters *v-i* thread their way at a great pace, each following the other's thread, through the life or the vision of a *je vis*—"*je vis des lettres,*" she says—and the speed, which is still the speed of what she calls "letters of omnipotence" ("notes at high speed"), I will have to, as is too often the case, alas, isolate a fragment, here in the body [*corps*] of *OR.*

I will always do so while trembling, anxious not to cut while cutting out, not to tamper with the body of the text, even if I were a dexterous and respectful surgeon. Let us only attempt to isolate, for a furtive moment, in a dark room, an image, just a spectral outline, in order to try and see better inside, by radioscopy or radiography—let us cite therefore as a radiologist and not as a surgeon. But these rays, whatever precautions one may take, are not innocent and without danger, both for the radiologist whom I pretend to replace and for what he thus exposes to this sight of the invisible. Since all this then is not without high risk and not without violence, I will beg you, I will implore you to cancel my operation straightaway, in order to forget it and return the fragment thus localized by abstraction to the infinite differentiated immensity of the living body of the work, according to its/her sublime punctuation. Nobody, need I repeat, can compete with her when it comes to a genius for, and meticulous calculation of, punctuation—which is, one can never say this enough, the heart and as it were the living breath, the very lungs of the writing. Here punctuation removes itself or gets spirited (away) [*s'enlève elle-même*] by a punctual depunctuation of its very breath, in other words its life, its rhythm, its time, and precisely, its speed. The steady slowness with which *I* proceed and which is my *tempo,* the step of my insistence, will only trail [*traîner*], like the train of a dress [*traîne*] or a trail [*traînée*], behind the truly choreographic grace, the aerial evolution, the inspiredness of a writing that dances and sings ceaselessly. By raising all the points of its punctuation.

Now [*or*] toward the end of *OR*, would that you might read these live words [*mots en vie*], by which I was tempted to try my luck at a salutation and a salvation [*tenter . . . la chance d'un salut*] to begin with: the chance of my salvation, the salvation that I owe and which we probably all owe Hélène Cixous here today. Do we owe it to her? Yes, but this salvation that I owe her, I do not feel like laboring the point that I owe it to her—one does not owe a salvation any more than a grace. This language of debt was between us, from the beginning, irrelevant and measure-less, out of proportion. In addressing these words of recognition to her today by way of a salutation, for a salvation, I propose that we should rather, simultaneously, hear ourselves [*nous entendre*] receiving them from her, let these words of salutation and salvation come from her, agree and know how to [*nous entendre à*] receive them from her: in a word, hear and understand [*entendre*] the salutation/salvation, the name *salut*, as if given by her, in a doubly verbal fashion, by conjugating once again the homonymy of two gestures and two verbs: the *salut* that salutes and the *salut* that saves.

Now in the passage that I will end up reading, the *salut* that saves is called twice by its name. Twice it is said, always to the letter and with regard to the letter: "one is lost, saved," then "one is already saved."[68]

We had just heard about life and might, of "mighty lives" and "letters of omnipotence," of a life and a might that are basically *the same*. Might does not occur to life, it is not lacking from life as a predicate could be attributed and occur to or be lacking from a subject, as if one could say: here life is mighty, there it lacks might. No, life *is* mighty might, more or less mighty, differentially, but always mighty might. At least in her (skillful) address. What does that mean? I hear, in her [*chez elle*], the term *puissant* like a verb, rather than a predicative adjective, like the (discreet but effective and incontestable) grammatical inauguration of a new present participle as active as an active volcano. *Puissant* already probably bears in its grammatical normality, in its spelling, the memory of a Latin present participle (*potens* or *potentissimus*) for the verb *pouvoir*: certainly, is powerful what is possible [*est puissant ce qui peut*]. But here, in the (skillful) address of which I speak, it is as if one had to invent a new grammar, add a new present participle to this singular subjunctive modality, which in French is said *puisse*; henceforth *puissant* will not signify *pouvant* [being able to], from *pouvoir*, but *puissant*, from *puisse*, from *puisse* onward [*depuis "puisse"*]; not a present participle for *pouvoir*, no matter how little [*si peu*], nor for any *peut* whatsoever, but, according to some heresy of the subjunctive, an originary subjunctive, an equally present participle for *puisse*. *It is necessary* [il faut] (it all depends on the order or the promise, the performative injunction of the *il faut*) not only that the living of life *might* and *might be able to*; but also that what I here call life for her be, might be also what, beyond any ontology, any constative discourse on *what is*, on what one knows it is [*sait que c'est*], may *force* a movement that, without being, and according to a good deal of violence to the French language—her French language or mine here, I no longer know and it does not matter—yes, without being, allies the present participle to the subjunctive modality of the order or of the promise: *mighting* [puissant] so that this *might* [puisse], with a view that this *might*, such that this *might* and come about *in might* [en puissance].[69] But also in actuality, the *en puissance* here no longer designating the virtuality, the potentiality, a *dynamis* that one could traditionally continue to oppose to *energeia*. No, what arrives according to this mighty power of the "might," of the "would that it, he, or she might," really actually arrives, in real life. It is life for life. This grammatical alchemy makes the mighty power of the letter work and grants might not from power, having or being, but from the wish of the *puisse*, this wish that is an order, an "I order (*jubeo*)." That this *might* come about, therefore, from the jussory, the jussive, as the speech act theorists would say, the *jouissif*, as I would say, of an order or a plea that enjoys [*jouissent*] and jubilates already feverishly from the arrival that is thus commanded, of a "might" [*puisse*] ("would that you might live," "that this might happen/arrive," "would that you might hear me," "would that you might write," "would that I might receive the order to live," "would that the letter might arrive," and so on, always imminently, on the spot, in a moment [*sur l'heure et tout à l'heure*]). You would not be able to derive the "might" in and by whose address one accedes to thought and to the effectiveness of might. It is not the modality of a verbal tense among others. Nor is it a secondary semantic determination of the verb and the noun *pouvoir, possum, potis sum, dynamis,* potentiality, possibility. *Puisse,* on the contrary, is the quasi-underivable trace that one must presuppose *so* that the other agencies (for example, power, *posse, dynamis,* dynasty, potentiality, then act and effectiveness) *might,* precisely, appear. Hence speed, the quasi-infinite speed of tautology I was speaking of just now. (Deleuze, I think, a long time ago, was able to remark on a certain speed in an article on Hélène Cixous. I no longer remember what he says about it, but I remember that the vertiginous speed had not escaped him—or that he had not escaped it.)[70] The speed of which I am speaking and will speak again is not only a certain rhythm of the writing, its lively address or the vivacity of its furtive agility—even though this is also the issue and the greatest danger, for a lazy reading lies therein, be it academic or journalistic criticism: this criticism will have to be taught—and this will take a long time—to read very slowly, this speed that never dispenses you from one step at a time, the marked pause from interval to interval, from syllable to syllable, from letter to letter, according to a punctuation at once strict and free, in all the detours of a musical, reflecting labyrinth of composition, inside each book—each book is a world, a monad, a life, the forgetting of all the others—and from one book to the next—each book keeps the reflexive, wakeful, yet elliptical memory of so many others, including her own. The speed of which I am speaking, and will speak again, not only characterizes the relation between time and space in a movement that would affect a body, for example the body of a letter when it moves in order to go from one point to another in space or time, on the page, for example, or between pages, or between dreaming and awakening, phantasm and reality, one language and the other, one figure of the other and another, in short, the genius for substitution. That is speed, of course, but not only that. The speed of which I am speaking is even faster than all these speeds; it is mightier than them, omnipotent since it is the quasi-infinite acceleration inside the "might." No sooner said than done: for that it is enough that life, that which is still called life (and which we will attempt to think), might make-let come the order of the "might." But the order of the "might," that which belongs to the order of the "might," contains the order of the "I order" (*jubeo*, the jussory or jussive, the *jouissif*) as well as, simultaneously, the wish, the plea, the desire: one can no longer distinguish between the imploring of an entreaty and the intractable authority of the command; therein lies the living genius of the "might." It is enough therefore that life might make-let come the order of the "might." And that with all the mildness required, it should always be giving an order. Still it needs to be possible [*qu'elle le puisse*], and that is the tautology of might: still it needs to be possible for it to desire, want, command, plead, make a wish—and therefore *pronounce* this "might," pronounce it aloud or in a low voice, pronounce it while uttering it or without uttering it, with or without words. It is therefore necessary and sufficient that life might let-make come "might," so that the subject and the object of the "might," if you want, might happen/arrive. That is the infinite speed of this mighty tautology. It is sufficient that I might really, mightily say, "Would that the letter might arrive" and the letter is already here [*là*], around here [*par ici*], around there [*par là*] even, has somehow arrived: without delay, without causing me delay. For just as I am/follow [*suis*] the address, I am/follow the letter addressed to me. This will be said in the golden words of *OR* a bit further, a few pages later, in the same breath of three sentences I will be glossing later. They say: "I write to you. Yes of course I say, I am/follow your letter. I am/follow myself your letter to me I say." (And the "yes" you have just heard, "Yes of course I say, I am/follow your letter . . . ," answers the other, but it breathes and murmurs, I'll come back to this, in *je suis* as, and as much as, *je puisse*).

Let us not act as if, speaking of absolute speed, we could say: I know what speed, the essence of speed, is. Or as if it only helped us pose the question "what is speed?" otherwise. No, we only accede to this experience of an unobjectivizable and unformalizable differential of speed, of a pure changing of gear—namely, that the question "what is speed?" and any possible answer to this question, in the form of *this is that*, arrives at a certain speed: it is already outsped by a speed. Speed itself, the speed in question in the question "what is speed?" is overtaken by speed [*prise de vitesse*], as one says taken by surprise, taken with somebody [*éprise*], or drunk from taking too much wine [*prise de vin*], intoxicated with speed, while slowness itself merely modalizes the possibility of an acceleration and therefore of a changing of gear. The changing of gear is the lever of might, even might itself. There is no *essence* of speed, nor a metalanguage, nor a theorem for it, outside this differential. There is no essence, only a mighty power of speed.

The speed of which we are speaking, even *before* being, *earlier than* [plus tôt que] being anything identifiable whatsoever, and in order to be what it also is in this case, namely the figure of a certain relation between time and movement in a race that displaces a moving body from one point to the other, before being, earlier than being and in order to be the animation and elation, the rhythm of a sentence, its pulse and heartbeat, its breathing or its tachycardia, before being and in order to be what it is in fact, namely a speed of displacement in writing—well, speed should change its name because it operates this rhythmic or spatio-temporal *displacement* only by beginning with *replacement*. Before displacing, it replaces. If it displaces so quickly, it is because it replaces. This is why it is infinite, or absolute, like an acceleration that goes faster than speed: even before moving and being able to move [*pouvoir mouvoir*], it replaces, it substitutes, it puts in the place of (one address for another, a word, a phoneme, a grapheme for another, one meaning for another), it changes subjects, it replaces the subject, identity, gender [*sexe*], or language itself. Absolute speed, the speed that absolutely economizes on speed, is first of all the relation to oneself as the relation to the other of a metonymy or a homonymy that *replaces* a noun, a mark, the address, or the meaning of a phoneme, of a syllable, or of a grapheme, etc., instantly, at once, without delay. Replaces them on the spot [*sur place*], at once [*sur l'heure*], and forthwith [*sur-le-champ*]. This ab-

solute economy of speed is an *eco-homonymy* or an *ecometonymy* or
an *eccehomonymy*. If this logic is also a logic of the mighty power
of eventhood, it is because the replacement lies precisely in taking the place, in *taking place*, therefore in taking place in the very
replacement which, receiving the place, gives place [*qui donne lieu
en recevant le lieu*], and opening, lets the place open itself; it lets/
makes the open place come about through the replaceability of the
irreplaceable itself. The speed of replacement is the very placement
of what is called an event, in its absolute inaugurality. Inside the
mark, the event replaces itself; this is a speed whose proposition
is as tautological as it is heterological. But as this speed always
remains a differential *econohomonymy* of the might, it also watches
over the race, the changes of pace and the laws of substitution
of all imaginable racing vehicles, no matter how heterogeneous
they may be, for example, between the conscious ego and the unconscious, between all the places of the psychic apparatus, all the
subject agencies and all the names (me and the author, the fathers,
my mother, and me, my brother and me, my sex and the other
sex, etc.). All these places and all these agencies have a different
tachycardia but they are replaceable within the same economy of
speed, the same tautoheterologic of the event, of a *taking place*
that at once pardons like an act of grace [*comme une grâce graciée*],
gives time and interrupts the course of normal time, makes history in interrupting it with a revolution: in the instantaneity of
the instant, at once [*sur l'heure*], on the spot. And this takes place
underneath, in a submarine fashion, between the underside of the
*sub*junctive and the underside of *sub*stitution.

Everything happens therefore as if I proposed or decreed around
here, presuming or exceeding an authority, that from now on in
the French language, the words *puissant* and *puissance* would no
longer be formed from a nominalized present participle, that is
from the complement of an actual power, or even of virtual potentiality. *Puissant, puissante, puissance* would henceforth be written
otherwise, according to another grammar, from her own signature,
that of a *puisse* awaiting its countersignature. *Puissance* would come
from, and partake of, *puisse* and not elsewhere. My decisional in-

vention would be one of these countersignatures, which would not only inscribe themselves on the very body of a given language that would be its support. The countersign would change the very body of the given language, its semantics and its grammar.

Then, of course, as has often been said, a letter can also not arrive, it is always possible. But this then means that the mighty power of the "might" has not arrived to itself. It will not have been mighty enough. *Lively* enough, and therefore fast enough. And this can always happen [*arriver*]. For the might in question, I insist, has to do with a differential and is nothing outside itself. It is therefore *finite*. Besides, as we will see, just as the possible is not on the other side, on the side opposed to the impossible, impotence is equally not the opposite of might or potency; it is impotence itself that makes the impossible and that becomes omnipotent. There are not two sides, therefore there is no side, and that is the undecidable. And that all this would be intimately linked with infinite speed, with a speed that is so much faster than speed that it is no longer speed but only the homonymy of speed, which therefore can just as well go very slowly, no one says it all better and faster than herself, for example, in *Jours de l'an* shortly after the Rilke passage (already from one side to the other) that I quoted a moment ago:

> . . . she becomes the Angel of the Nonencounter. What delights me is this slow speed, this potency in impotence [*puissance d'impuissance*] from which we may only obtain pleasure [*jouissance*] on the streets of our dreams.[71]

"The streets of our dreams": you know that she writes by dream,[72] if I may say so, as one would say to navigate by sail or wind, by drawing energy as well as the figures of her writing from a phantasmoneiric flux that—and this is its miracle and its magic—is not interrupted by awakening, at the moment when the most impeccably wakeful vigil [*veille*] causes her writing to be the most closely watched [*surveillée*], the most accomplished, the most skillfully composed, in its atomic grain and its main musical, rhythmic, narrative, theatrical, and of course tropic, semantic, and thematic units. Here again, and I will say this just as naively as I think, I do not know any other example of such a miraculous alliance between night and day, between the mad turbulence of the dream and the calculating culture of the literal and literary realization. (Let me say in parenthesis, once again, since it is agreed that I will not be speaking of myself, I believe my eyes all the less, in front of this miracle, since I, who am still on the other side, work on the contrary by dream's interruption, more or less, and I write when *my* awakening, unlike her own awakenings, I suppose, when my first awaking begins by turning off the current of the phantasm and putting an end to the night. The phantasm can then cut a path through what I write only unbeknownst to myself, without my authorization: I betray my dreams, in the double sense of the word "betray": I abandon them, I leave them and let them come back only in the guise and disguise of symptoms, which in turn betray, belie, and deny me. I am therefore in betrayal in all respects. I live and write (on) it [*j'en vis et j'en écris*]. She does not; another element, another way, she has the power and the grace to authorize her dreams. Therefore, her dreams, because she remains faithful to them, are consecrated, enfranchised, and ready to enter writing [*entrer en écriture*],[73] to be admitted into the holy orders of writing [*entrer dans l'ordre et dans les ordres de l'écriture*], *authorized* as author's dreams, as one says author's privilege, author's signature, author's copyright, author's correction. To be on the other side, for me, means being at once less conscious and less unconscious than her. Therefore less fast as well. I close the parenthesis.)

This mighty tautology that knows how to make the address itself arrive,[74] can always be called magic, incantation, animism, phantasm of omnipotence. Certainly, but this baptism is no use as long as one has not clarified what these words mean: magic, the soul or the spirit of animism, telepathy, telephony, phantasm and especially the phantasm of omnipotence, and above all the relation between the phantasm and the event, and especially what *happens* or *arrives* with the phantasm. For what is at stake, in other words, is a new logic of the phantasm and of the event that, inseparable from a poetics of the event, may take into account an unheard-of, performative might, a mighty power of making-say as making-happen or arrive, which speech act theory will not get the better of and whose possibility it has probably not yet objectivized. More precisely, such a might is no longer contained within the classical philosophical concept of "possibility," *dynamis, possibilitas,* in the traditional modality of the possible or of the virtual that is traditionally opposed to the act, the real, or the necessary. The philosophical concept of might, as one most frequently interprets it, is not powerful enough here; it is not capable of this might. *This* might, *her* might, is not virtual, certainly, but its actuality, for this might is actual if it decides to act, is not a matter of actuality or activity, of *energeia* that is opposed to *dynamis.*

Instead of going further in this direction, I will say that such a transmutation of the letter and of the verbal moods is everywhere at work in her, in particular, and this is it, in the term *vis,* which initiates the series of words *vie, vivre, vision, vitesse,* and so many others, but which is first declined as the past of a *vision* ("*Je vis des lettres* [I saw letters]," she says in the past historic tense, as we will hear in a moment) and equally as the present of the verb *vivre,* "*Je vis des lettres* [I live on letters]," in the present tense, or like an order given to the other, a plea or an effective (*felicitous*) injunction, to the other or to oneself: "live," "would that you might live" and *listen* to these words (listen, obey!), and it is then, at the end of this magic or by the grace of this letter, life, or survival in potentiality [*en puissance*].

I have just said "magic," "speed," "life," "telepathy or telephony." I will slow down my pace again and dwell a little in the vicinity of these words and what sustains them with such and such occurrences in the last-born of her books, *OR,* which I am treating here, for lack of time, as a metonymy of all the others. I will probably speak directly (I will explain myself in a moment) only of the first and the last of the books published to date by Hélène Cixous. Which is most unjust, for, even if *Le Prénom de Dieu* and *OR* have a metonymic thrust and stand *for* the entire work, each book is a singular and irreplaceable living entity. Each book has a (hi)story, each book is a unique (hi)story and living breath, which then command an absolute and absolutely solitary reading. Each book is a beginning, including the one called *Les Commencements*. And this is why it is always necessary to begin again with her. Each book has a proper noun; it would be a crime to speak of it only metonymically, to call it by the name or in the name of another. For a metonymy can also kill. Each book has a proper noun, each work is a proper noun, or indeed a filiation of proper nouns, even when the name, or indeed the noun of the name or of the first name, does not appear, as it does on the other hand in titles such as *Le Prénom de Dieu* (in the singular) (1967) or *Prénoms de personne* (in the plural) (1974) or *Révolution pour plus d'un Faust* (1975), *Le Nom d'Oedipe* (1978), even when a proper noun does not appear as such, whereas it sometimes does, when the title, which is itself a name, bears a mythical proper noun (*Oedipus* or *Faust*) or a real proper noun: *Joyce* (1968), *Pierre Goldman* (1975), *Dora* (1976), *Norodom Sihanouk* (1985), *Clarice Lispector* (1989), *Beethoven . . .* (1993), the most lively and the most fictive of all, one of whose praises lies in saying, again at the moment of Betrayal, that within its "rounded slowness" "gathers a superhuman speed."

Even when a proper noun and a proper forename do not appear in the title, each book puts to work the act of a proper and properly singular naming. *OR* is obviously the fragment of a proper noun, of so many proper nouns, starting with Georges. This is also why, apart from reasons of economy, I had decided to speak only of two books, in order merely to half-name, between two (hi)stories of names, the first, before the name (*Le Prénom de Dieu*, the forename of "Side"—remember that God will later be synonymous with *Side* with a capital *S*), and the most recent, after the name, according to the name, *OR*. Therefore each book is absolutely alone, it is a beginning that is as absolute as a proper noun, even if, however, a vast hall of echoes and mirrors, the labyrinth of so many tangled-up threads turns these solitary books, which are irreducible the one to the other, across so many generations, into a single genealogical and elemental signature, that is to say, greater than itself. Nothing will be able to justify the limits of the reading I propose today, save the decency that forces me not to keep you for too long, listening to me rather than to her, a decency that goes together with the wish or the order that I dare pronounce: would that *you* might read her, as *I* think it must be done, infinitely.

So I have just said, as I was saying and am now repeating, "magic," "speed," "life," and "telepathy or telephony." With slow steps I will approach these words, what sustains them with such and such occurrences in the last-born, the latest of her books, *OR*. Now [*or*] as early as the beginning of *OR*, long before the passage with which I began, the thought of "magic" was simultaneously tied to life, more precisely to the order that says, in the imperative: "Live [*vis*]," but which says it in monosyllabic fashion (you have noticed that we mostly speak of monosyllables, like *si, puisse,* and *vis, la vie* or the order *vis,* the present or past historic tense *je vis*), and, being tied to life for life, this thought of magic was betting on the absolute economy of an absolute speed, namely the telegraphic, what she will call the *telegraphic injunction.* The telegraphic is what goes as fast as possible, in the transport of short words, reduced to the minutest length and weight, the winged flight of short, furtive, agile, and light terms. The telegram goes as fast as possible, as far as possible, while telephony is here merely telegraphy to the nth power. I will read the fragments of a sequence in which I will emphasize a few words without commenting on them. The sequence, at the beginning of *OR*, comes shortly after the passage about "my uncle Freud" in italics (of which I will speak again in a moment and whose return I am preparing myself). Freud *sings* while telling a dream. Now as soon as "my uncle Freud" stops singing the "song of enchantment" ("singing the song of enchantment," these are the words of *OR*, and the mighty power of the *might* of which we are speaking, as of Hélène Cixous's poetics in fact, is the enchantment, the arrival as if by an enchantment, where the poetic song, the charm, the *carmen,* and magical power are allied to *kommen lassen,* make come in letting come, if one insists on formulating in the language of the mother or of the uncle this formula of the miracle of a chant of enchantment, which is also a song of songs), as soon as Freud has fallen silent, and after the end of the italics, here is the passage in which I will merely emphasize a few words (I will write them silently on the board):

But one must not forget the name.

I forget everything, as is well known, but when it comes to **telephone** numbers I have an anomaly. I have the **magical** names in my fingertips. All the ones I keep in my fingers are protected.

This is a serious **power** but it is not reserved for me. So that a person rises from the dead [Lazarus will pay a visit to the text on the following page—JD] it is necessary to catch the ghost by a **wisp** [**mèche**] **of life** [this *mèche* is a lock of hair, of course, a piece given or kept of the other's body—and you will see it metamorphosed, as if by an enchantment, into a telephone wire, a braid of name, the wire of a funambulist or of a trapeze artist; but the wisp of life also resembles the flame of a candle that holds on to the soul of the departed who is named in the following sentence—JD]. Besides one cannot catch up with the long departed for they are totally dead, there is no point **calling** then. The resurrection **calls** are addressed to the people who died recently for they still remain between two doors for about eight days. Maybe a fortnight. During these days it is still possible to bring them back to this side.[75]

So without commenting on this passage, which I am going to continue to read in a moment anyway, I will only note the possible (and, according to me, decisive) signification of this double insistence: first on the surrectional—insurrectional and resurrectional—efficacy of the appellation: the nomination is *at once* a noun and a verb, a word and an act, an act *that makes the name* but also a gesture *that the name makes*; this first insistence is inseparable from an insistence also on the limited time of the vigil, of waking, on the finite duration of this magical power. What does this finitude of time and of resurrectional power mean? That in all this, which comes and comes back, it is a question of life and not death, of a differential power of finite life over life that stays alive, keeps itself alive, comes back to life. There is no side for death, this is what finitude here means, paradoxically; what comes around here, on this side, from the rib/shore [*côte*] or the side [*côté*], which is only the side of life, is living life. Consequently, what attempts resurrection "between two doors during eight days" (a detail that connotes probably a rite and a rhythm of mourning in a Jewish family: the psychic breath of the living survives and floats, is still animate for a certain time after death), what decides here *for life* is not a wish for immortality or eternity, at least in the accepted sense of these two words, which will therefore have to be swiftly changed in a moment. For this appellation, which catches the ghost by a wisp of life, there is a time of survival that is life itself, life in life (a life that is no more death than the opposite of death, a life that does not know death), but there is neither immortality nor eternity, in the old sense of these words—unless [*sauf si*] the unharmed [*sauf*] being, the spared [*sauve*] and thus pardoned [*graciée*] life, in its finite moment of life, deserves to be called immortality or eternity, in the grace of the finite instant; and it is probably this appellation of life that we are and will still be enchanted by, an appellation of life that knows equally neither death nor immortality, namely eternity outside time. Everything takes place in the instant. Time is this mighty power imminent from "at the moment [*sur l'heure*]" to "in a moment [*tout à l'heure*]" at full tilt [*à toute allure*] (she so loves the moment [*heure*], she is all for the moment [*toute à l'heure*] to such an extent that I almost entitled this talk on might "*Toute à l'heure*," with *toute* in the feminine of course). The mighty power of *toute à l'heure* is the power to take off in the infinite acceleration of the appellation. I resume my quotation:

> . . . for about eight days. Maybe a fortnight. During these days it is still possible to bring them back **to this side**. Obviously it is necessary that certain delicate conditions be fulfilled: at stake is the **vital bond** that unites two creatures . . .

This vital bond will be metamorphosed as if by an enchantment: from the lock of hair into a telephone wire, into a "telephone cord," into a telegraphic and, therefore, telepathic wire, into a "braid of name" or into the wire of a funambulist or of an acrobatic trapeze artist. The thread of this "vital bond" is the mighty power of life, it is nothing else than life for life, in that it binds to life, which is nothing but this engagement that binds life to itself—and to nothing else: the verb "bind" binds itself tautologically to life, it goes and has meaning only for life, it binds life,

which binds itself to itself, at the very point where, in this powerful bond that it weaves with itself and which it therefore is, it is
attached to itself [*tient à elle-même*] only by a hair—but by a hair
of the other, who is none other than a mad trapeze artist, himself
hanging [*se tenant*] above the abyss, without a net, by a thread or
by a hair.

> . . . at stake is the **vital bond** that unites two creatures, a bond of
> which one may think that it is symbolic since it is so imperceptible
> or transparent, but which exists in reality, as those who belong to the
> **tribe of the connected** [**raccordés**] can testify . . .

The "tribe of the connected,"[76] which should probably be added
to the tribes of Israel, is the tribe of those who recognize one another, in accordance with this filiation of the thread [*filiation du fil*]
of hair, of the telephone wire or the funambulist's wire, and who
are connected as one is connected to a writing line or a telephone
line, connected to the "living telephone cord" that will come up in
the following sentence, but also in tune [*raccordés*] with the musical chord [*accord*] of the enchantment, of the song of songs, and
always connected by the heart.

> . . . as those who belong to the tribe of the connected can testify.
> This extensible hair, a kind of nerve, behaves like a living telephone
> cord. The essential orders, only imperatives, pass through this **thread**
> [**fil**] drawn between two souls, as if the thread only supported a few
> telegraphic injunctions. It is men who make sentences. God speaks in
> syllables like animals. Divine yelps: the soul barks the other soul reacts
> as if to an electric shock. Come! Be! Stay! Live!

I suspend the quotation here for a moment, at the point where
we have just heard these imperatives, which are might itself and
pass on the phrase of the human voice; they exceed it with the
voicing of the injunction: "Come! Be! Stay! Live!"; each time these
are short translations or, at an absolute speed, monosyllabic and
metonymic equivalents of "might [*puisse*]." All these orders call
implicitly but necessarily upon the mighty power of the *might*. We
must also take the word "soul" (" . . . the soul barks the other soul

reacts as if to an electric shock . . . ") seriously each time. Here it too finds itself awakened to the youthfulness of its omnipotence. For it not only tells of life, the breath of the living, namely the psyche, this other thought *for life* that we are attempting to sense here. The animated breath of the *psyche*, or of the spirit, of the *pneuma* (the telegraphic also remains the pneumatic), is also of course what blows without delay or relay through the telephonic voice in according itself with the cord of the "living telephone"— and the soul breathes or inspires only where telepathic telephony operates. However animated and animal it needs to remain (I will speak of animism in a moment), through the memory of all the dogs that fill this passage—"the soul barks the other soul reacts as if to an electric shock," without punctuation, as if "barks" was immediately transitive and as if the other soul was barked by the soul that barks, that barks it [*l'aboie*], the soul drinks it [*la boit*] as other, without swallowing it: it addresses the other in touching and making the other answer or respond without delay, the name and the address of the other co-responding [*correspondant*] at/to the end of his address, at/to the end of the line—this soul that is as spiritual as it is animal, as animal as it is divine, is not, as one would often like to think, alien to technique and to electricity, and its "might" partakes of what in English is simply called "power," electricity as *power*. The *puisse* is electrical: *may, might, and power*, the instantaneity of e-mail, of the naked voice of electronic mail ("Divine yelps: the soul barks the other soul reacts as if to an electric shock . . . "). But above all the monosyllabic brevity of these calls, these "telegraphic injunctions," these "divine yelps" ("Come! Be! Stay! Live!") does give us to think that this thought of the soul, of the *psyche*, the *pneuma*, of life or of animal breath, is nothing but this enacted thought of might, namely of absolute speed that makes the letter arrive before the letter. This telepathic phone call joins the other, it comes and goes at least as fast as or maybe faster than light, at the speed of what in any case, according to the voice, *(sur)renders itself* [se rend] blindly, without a necessary need for visibility, to the greatest possible distance, that of the other wher-ever he may be. Outspeeding speed, this is an infinite acceleration that needs animal or divine monosyllabism. This acceleration, this monosyllabic condensation, this telegraphic injunction as quasi-interjection, clamor of exclamation, mere exclamation mark (come! be! stay! live! yes [*sí*]! there [*là*]! two pages later, it will be "Lazarus! Get out! Come here! Come forth! . . . "), this "claim," this exclamation that claims, would be the very *essence* of the soul, if the movement of this mighty power, the primordiality of the "might" from which this power can do what it can do, was not older than the essence, precisely, than being and ontology, than the utterance "it is" in the form S is P: *c'est.* (We will see later how the *for* of *for life* begins by upsetting the authority of the "it is," of the essence, of the "what life is.") The *might* of this mighty power *is not.* It goes so fast, it comes so fast, even before light and the *phainesthai*, before being, before the phenomenality of what appears, that it is nothing; since it has, keeps, or remains this mighty power, and provided that it might [*pourvu qu'il la puisse*], the "might" [*le "puisse," la "puisse"*] carries beyond being, *might by making* [puisse par faire] being, letting or making be what is. Before wondering about some essence of the soul, of the spirit, or of being, it is probably necessary to think the soul and being from the "might," the "fiat" whose jussive or *jouissif* subjunctive is at the very origin of Hélène Cixous's world. I carry on with my suspended quotation and emphasize once again.

> Come! Be! Stay! Live! So it is that the will is also a physical phenomenon it wants-must [*veut-doit*] gather all the **vital** currents of the will into a single crucial point . . .

"Wants-must gather," "wants-must" in one hyphenated word. Want-must [*vouloir-devoir*]: wanting is a *must*, a necessity and an injunction, therefore at once the absolute activity of wanting and the faithful or passive obedience of an order. The will listens, it is a will to listen—and, like the telephone, it is also the condition of reading as much as of writing. It is rare, precarious, and threatened like the mighty power of life.

Here again, the vital, the live-ance of life [le *vivement de la vie*], before and beyond being, gathers itself, "wants-must gather itself," as she says, into a single indivisible point in space, "into a single crucial point" (this may be one of the crossroads in a work that gathers us together here),[77] into a single crucial point, like the monosyllabic punctuality of the "Come!" or "Live!" just now, the punctuality of the exclamation mark or of the appellation mark. The infinite speed of the "Live!" or "Come!" must contract everything, and I do mean contract, according to the contraction that contracts and to the contract that we can see coming: it "wants-must" contract into a monosyllable or into a point. The monosyllabic exclamation is the time of this point; but since the other is what is at stake and since this point, however indivisible it may be, is not closed in on itself like a fist, the art of punctuation, which will never stop amazing me, is also an art and an ethics of punctuality. As will be said so well in the two following paragraphs, it calls for a wager [*gage*], a commitment [*engagement*] of the other, at both ends of the line and of the lifeline. This is why the "single point" is said to be "crucial." The word "crucial" signals less toward the cross than toward the decisive test, toward the crossroads of passion itself, between life and death, in a (hi)story that does not exclude loss, but which on the contrary implies the moment of kenosis and abandonment. Because abandonment, the "why are you forsaking me?" is possible, the punctuality of the point is crucial. In a mighty power of life as a mighty power of resurrection. Next paragraph, new line, as one comes near the telephone.

In the gap between two doors those whom we wrongly call dead are in the simplified state of a microscopic eardrum. If there is a **bond** then [the "vital bond" of a moment ago—JD], and if **from both sides** one wants to resuscitate [one never resuscitates alone, one resuscitates from both sides—JD]—and of course if the **contract** between the two people is still in full force, but this goes without saying [this "this goes without saying," this "that is to say," which goes without saying, is the absolute of contraction, the infinite acceleration of the monosyllabic punctuality to the point of silence and the unsaid—JD]—then **a return to life** is possible.

All this requires a purity of the two souls that cannot bear the slightest exemption. Both must want it and have faith without trembling without hidden thoughts without thought . . .

The voice says: "Want . . . and have faith. . . . " Here again, instant telescoping, punctual syncope of two apparently opposite movements, will and faith. Arriving from both sides, from the one and the other, the two movements contract into a single one, indistinctly: active or decisional will is no longer opposed to faith, which abandons itself blindly to the other without defense, without hidden thoughts, incalculably—and that is the moment of omnipotence. She starts on the next line, and it is a single paragraph over two lines or two threads:

> An acrobatic act of trapeze artists who have never touched a trapeze in their history.

After this flight of trapeze artists, from this duo of trapeze artists, one jumps, across a blank of more than one line, to the following paragraph. I am going to read it too in order to release the mighty power of some of its terms, for example "life," "visa," "visit," but first the "braid" in the "braid of name," the "greeting" in "the name of a person that greets me," the "pact" with my cat, a pact that works through a "pronunciation," relays the "contract between two people," which we have just read and which is inscribed in a scene that had begun not with the cat but with the dog, all this, all this life happening between cat and dog [*entre chien et chatte*][78] therefore; and then especially a certain "yes I will yes," which will be no less important to me in a moment because it relaunches Molly's final affirmation, at the end of *Ulysses* ("and yes I said yes I will Yes"), than by what follows and says "and each time it is for the whole of life."

This "it is for the whole of life," I did not read or reread it, in any case I did not recognize it until long after choosing my title. I will explain myself in a moment, when I begin to say at last how and why, according to me, even more than the "might," or in alliance with it, it is the enigma of this "for" that makes thought itself tremble in the expression "it is *for* life." As if it were necessary to think life, the mighty power of life, from "for" and not the reverse; as if in the expression "for life" one should above all not believe to be first assured of the meaning of "life," which one would then decline in a syntagm in the dative. No, the word "life," the most common word there is, the only word that carries enough weight faced with being (so much so that in the philosophical gigantoma-chia, from Plato to Descartes, from Nietzsche to Husserl, Bergson and Heidegger, among others, the only big question whose stakes remain undecided would be to know whether it is necessary to think being [*l'être*] before life, entity [*l'étant*] before the living or the reverse), well, the word "life" would not be thinkable in its meaning, it would not announce itself before what, grammatically, gives itself as a preposition, namely "for." It would therefore be necessary for us first to surrender to a subjunctive (*might*) and to a preposition (*for*), long before the infinitive, the indicative or the name of being, not to mention the proposition "it is [*c'est*]," "S is P," "this is that," in response to the question of what must be known or stated: "What is it?" This "for," this *pro-* would become the prolegomenon of everything, it would be said before any *logos*, it goes in all directions, that of finality or of destination, of the gift, donation and dativity, but also of substitution and replacement: this *for* that, this one *in the place of* the other. In the place of: the one for the other. The law of speed. An absolute prerequisite, the *pro* of *for* thus pronames and prenames everything. As a great poet of substitution (I'll explain myself later perhaps), Hélène Cixous does not exercise her mighty power only in the art of the forename [*prénom*] (for example God's forename) or of the pronoun (for example, a person's pronoun [*pronom de personne*]). I would say, making up a word for her, that she fornames [*pournomme*] every-thing. As one would say that the French language has a taste *for* and relishes [*se pourlèche les lèvres*] all the words in *pour*, which will then find themselves awakened to their mighty power.

Why [*pourquoi*]? For what? For whom? I do not know, but pro-vided [*pourvu*] one knows how, in language, to read and write. But if "for" conditions the meaning of "life," it does not follow that it would define the ontological or transcendental condition of everything. This is not to recall, through a nominalization, that a certain indecomposable "being-for" would be more originary than anything else, the absolute origin of meaning. No, before the be-

ing-for, and even the being-of-life-for, there would be the life-for-
life, the *for-life*, which at once gives and replaces life with life in
view. And this is why, up to the end, "for life" has no end, it knows
no end. Everything happens on the side of "for," but I have not
yet done with wandering along [*côtoyer*] this strange shore that
one calls a side. This "for life" is not a *being* for life symmetrically
opposed to the famous *Sein zum Tode*, being-toward-death, as its
other side. It is on the same side. Besides, if we were given the
time, I would have relaunched a patient and difficult discussion
between this "for life" and the "being-toward-death" by coming
back from the side of the side, toward this passage in *Sein und Zeit*
(§49), which I interpreted in this very place six years ago. Against
the metaphysics of death, which are interested in the beyond, that
is to say in the other side (*Jenseits*), Heidegger recalls that one
must, on the contrary, methodically depart and remain *here on
this side*, on the side of *this* side, on the side of the here of the here
below (*das Diesseits*), the side from which only the gap emerges
between *das Diesseits* and *das Jenseits*, the Here below and the Beyond. The difference between the Here below of *this* side and the
Over-there, the Beyond on the other side, still appears only on
this side, on the side of *das Diesseits*. Before the difference between
this side and the other side, between here and over there, there is,
forever, an "on this *side*" (*das Diesseits*), which does not have to
be crossed—and, besides, cannot be. This is what Heidegger says.
Unfortunately, he does not call this "life," a life before the opposition between life and death. And above all, if one translates *Jenseits*
by "beyond" and *Diesseits* by "here below," as one always does,
this passage from the side [*côté*] to the shore [*côte*], by which this
whole geo-genealogy may have begun to wait for us, is lost, as it is
lost in German anyway. Finally, even if the "for life" that is being
analyzed here did not merely designate the other side symmetrically opposed to being-toward-death (*Sein zum Tode*), and if *life*
and *death* here were not antonyms, the semantic turbulence of this
verbal animal, "for," would certainly not let itself be translated,
exhausted, or comprehended by a *zu* or *zum*, which anyway is
itself difficult to translate into another language. Nor would there

be any equivalence, despite so many correspondences, between the *there* of the being-*there* of *Dasein* and the *there* [là] of *La*, which irradiates or irrigates H.C.'s text from all sides.

No, life *for* life (and not being-for-life) is therefore nothing else than a living of death, but yes, still living death, living it for oneself, for the other, and for life. Later we will call this experience, or even experimentation: living for the sake of living, and in order to see—what it feels like, just to try. She keeps trying, as we can hear still, always.

At this moment in *OR* an amorous beast passes, one of these "clockworked animals" that she says we are,[79] a sensual beast of which it is said, without punctuation, that it is "fast elegant absent-minded indefatigable human like a giant cat it is made so stubborn by desire that it does not see dying coming." But on the facing page, all the words in *or* (and *mort* [death] is one of them) ring into one another:

> . . . goes out. Out. Dead. Out dead death's out/fate death. The word's out/fate. The word dead/death. The fate of the words progress out/fate death. The flesh eaten alive. And with each breath it feeds the enemy. To live one dies.[80]

This "to live one dies" signs everything, it gathers all that remains to be said in a formula as sure and as open, as vacant and anonymous as it is general and elliptical. For, in this form, this risks being not only an abstract but also a false generality. Anyway, it is a true generality, save for exceptions, precisely. It is applicable only to the "one" of the "one says." And the exception is the dead-father. But it is a general exception since the irreplaceable dead-father, as we have heard, finds himself replaced, pluralized, metonymized. She calls herself the daughter of the dead-father*s*. This truth is in general and generally applicable to exception itself, it is applicable to everything that lives and dies ("to live one dies")—*save* for the unique father, Georges, who tears himself away from generality itself. He keeps himself out of the georgic or Adamic generality of the earth so as to return from it, to tear himself away from it, and he remains exception itself, the exception of the exception, the unique exception, the only proper noun, the one for whom the word "*sauf* [save, safe]" would have been as if invented. That is to say, poetically reinvented at the instant in order to be given to the French language from the other side, all the other sides of France. I attempted to show elsewhere that the word *sauf* leads back to the origin of faith and religion itself, of the sane [*sain*], the holy [*saint*] and the sacred, of the immunity of the unscathed (*heilig*, as her mother might say).[81]

She says:

> And with each breath it feeds the enemy. To live one dies. [New paragraph.—JD]
> But for my father it is different. He leaves safe.

That is to say: all this is true, yes, anonymously, to live one dies, save for my father, who remains safe, who leaves safe/save from life [*qui sort sauf de la vie*]. My father leaves life intact, he dies alive, unscathed, holy, untouched by death, he leaves life without dying the death [*mort*] that bites [*mord*] life. My dead father is not dead, bitten or eaten by death, and to say so is not a contradiction or a denial. It is the mightiest truth, the mightiest life.

I am skipping. She is skipping.

So, after the word "trapeze" ("An acrobatic act of trapeze artists who have never touched a trapeze in their history"), we skip a line before flying toward the following paragraph.

> But everything begins with the proper noun. I desire you, I keep you, I hold you steadily above the nothingness by your name; I pull you out of the grave by the braid of name. There is no small crime more hurtful to myself than to catch myself forgetting the name of a person who greets me.[82]

This "braid of name" no doubt weaves the "vital bond" that was mentioned above, just like the "extensible hair," the "living telephone cord," and the "thread drawn between two souls" we had just heard about. It is also the braid by which a trapeze artist holds the other by his name above the nothingness. But this braid also binds so many other things. Already naming itself, this braid of name, of the proper noun and of the common noun, does what it says and says what it is, namely the poetical operation of writing, which makes and lets the event come. It intertwines the most singular writing, the very operation of the text, what the text does as it writes the name (the text is a braid, a fabric interweaving these threads). It intertwines the braid *that* the text is with the braid *that* the text names, certainly, the "braid of name," but also, at the very passage of this braid, the most idiomatic and most irreplaceable there is (not only signed Hélène Cixous but signed in this unique passage, from one page to the next, only once), there it is, knotting itself and binding itself to the memory of all the immemorial braids, to the (hi)stories, the mythemes, the philosophemes, to all the tropes that not only twist and turn like braids but, immemorably, will have interwoven the (hi)story of the braid with the (hi)story of nomination, and the (hi)story of nomination with the (hi)story of generations or with the thread of filiations, in short, with history. The braid is the archive, public or secret, and one must have the secret even of the public one in order to decipher it. It is the absolute privilege, the mighty power of the poet or of the reciter. One could devote whole books to this archive, to this archive of the braid as a cryptic archive. To limit myself to a sole example of apparently the most distant and most deeply buried mythologies: I was rereading of late, as if by chance, Segalen's *Les Immémoriaux* (1907) on the Île de Groix. Right from the opening, entitled "The Reciter," Térii the Reciter, the "*Chief with the Grand Talk*," "would make up with great care these bundles of small ropes whose strands, stemming from a single little knotted bag"—the word used in French, *nouet*, is seldom used and almost extinct, and you will not find it in every dictionary; it belongs to the code of animal medicine or of magic, and it is used for a small knot of linen in which a substance can be boiled or infused. Let us only bear in mind that this word, itself rare, designates something that must be single or unique, "stemming from a single little knotted bag," Segalen writes: the knot around which the braid is formed, no matter how entangled, solid, and multiple it may be in the course of its linking to itself and to the other, must be irreplaceable; the *nouet*, the knot, the original ligament must be small, almost reduced to a point, and this small point must be absolutely unique. So the "Chief with the Grand Talk"

> . . . would make up with great care these bundles of small ropes whose strands, stemming from a single little knotted bag, spread out in various lengths broken up by knots at regular intervals. With his eyes shut, the Reciter would pick them apart one by one between his fingers. Each of the knots recalled the name of a traveler, a chief or a god, and all together they conjured up interminable generations. This braid was called "Origin-of-the-Word," for it seemed to bring about speech.

A little further on the same page comes the drama that can be presaged by, I quote, "the forgetting of the name," which is a "bad omen." I like to quote from this text here because it evokes at least, through the dimension of the braid (that is, the whole history of speech and names, all that happens and all the generations), not only the "braid of name" we have just come across in *OR* but also, weaving the metaphor or the metonymy, this immense braid that the work of Hélène Cixous is: through all the events of the world, on the stages of war and peace, of revolutions, of political, religious, and scientific cataclysms, an epic of generations unfolds or folds itself within it, is resolved and renewed [*s'y dénoue ou renoue*] with an amplitude and a delicacy in the stitching of which I know no other example. And since this braid of generations engenders as much as it registers, it displaces and replaces the places of the family, of what is called "my kinsfolk" [*les miens*] or "my family"—of what she herself sometimes calls so. We will see once more in a moment, among so many others, the shadow of a "Nuncle Freud" go by, of a certain "my nuncle Freud"—who had incidentally put forward on the topics of braiding, weaving, and femininity some imprudent propositions about which I showed, in *Un Ver à soie*, that Hélène Cixous had answered them in her own way, especially in *La* (1976).[83]

I first resume my quotation from *OR*:

> But everything begins with the proper noun. I desire you, I keep

you, I hold you steadily above the nothingness by your name; I pull you out of the grave by the braid of name. There is no small crime more hurtful to myself than to catch myself forgetting the name of a person who **greets** [**salue**] me. And the worst thing is that, if I ask this person whom I cannot keep in mind what their name is, then I execute them under their very eyes. But I did not want to kill the apparition of this person! Oh! No doubt I do not have enough of my blood to grant them, and under my eyes they remain among the shadows.

Between me and my cat the pact works through pronunciation . . .

I will still have to pronounce myself on this word "pronunciation" and all that it may mean. After this bond, this thread, or this cord, after the intertwining of this braid, which was *knotted* but also *named*, on the previous page, after the "contract between the two persons," here is the "pact with the cat." Contract, pact, bond, promise, wager. To say it too quickly in a word and to anticipate outrageously, what I would like to salute [*saluer*] by saying "H.C. *for* Life" is also this poem of the alliance, the event of this poetical alliance, of this betrothal, which works through an almost silent pronunciation between the two of them, of whom one no longer knows who speaks and who stays silent, who calls and who answers, who speaks at length and who, speaking little, speaks words of gold [*parle d'or*]. And "for life," "for the whole of life" will soon come in the same paragraph, in the same node [*nouet*]:

> Between me and my cat [says the reciter—JD] the pact works through pronunciation. Not only do I call her intensely, but each time there is also a betrothal between us; there is a demand that unites us in the timbre of my voice dwelling on her name. "Will you?" she hears and the rush of her body is a yes I will yes, and each time it is for the whole of life. I am fully aware of it, I never call out her name as I would toss a bit of fish.

I interrupt my quotation again, knowing full well how unfair and violent such interruptions are, but if I did not stop with this brutal regularity to announce each time what I will not do, namely to devote, as one should, several books to each sentence, to each theme, and to each program (for example, one among a thousand others, to the word "betrothal," which would require a significant reexamination of a field comprising over fifty books, poems, and plays, which are irrigated or magnetized to the letter by the betrothal, according to the letter in metamorphosis and metempsychosis of its word), if I did not interrupt these programmatic suggestions, then I would stay silent and simply say to you (what in truth I should be doing and am doing): read and reread everything yourselves, that is a job *for life*, and that will be just as well, you won't regret it; "for life" means also that: if you really want to read her and meet her, that is a job for life. I stop myself nevertheless in order to ponder, that is to say, meditate or premeditate a little this life, this name, the substitution of the irreplaceably unique Thessie and Molly, and this "bit of fish" (" . . . and the rush of her body is a yes I will yes, and each time it is for the whole of life. I am fully aware of it, I never call out her name as I would toss a bit of fish"). "The rush of her body is a yes I will yes, and each time it is for the whole of life": this does confirm that the pronunciation, the condition of the pact, as she was saying just now, does not have to be pronounced or literally uttered by a human voice. A movement of the body can pronounce a yes, decide with a yes, without saying yes. Thessie the cat can signify yes for life, like Molly, without saying yes like Molly.

First the "it is for the whole of life" of the "yes I will yes" is not merely a "once and for all" or once only for the whole of life; no doubt it is that, of course and therefore unreservedly (the life of this betrothal is the whole of life or it is nothing: life is first the whole of life). But that is to say also each time for the whole of life: the "yes" is each time unique and a rebeginning, as if it did not even have the memory of itself, which it keeps nonetheless. The "yes" of the "for the whole of life" is irreplaceable, at the very place and at the time of this irreplaceable invention of substitution that I will praise again in a moment. The "yes" is irreplaceable, like Messie or Thessie the cat, at the very moment when Molly's words are put in her mouth and when the pact struck with her recalls the "contract between the two persons" signed on the previous page.

The question remains that of the faith that, each time, allows the substitution of another time through an act of faith without altering the uniqueness of each time. And tying the knot of betrothal "for the whole of life" would be impossible—it remains in fact the impossible—like the faith that, believing in the other without believing in anything else, each time decides all the times in a single time without ever replacing one time by another. The event, and the poetics of the event we are attempting to think here, can only happen at this price: faith yet each time renewed [*la foi chaque fois toutefois*]. I would have liked to inscribe here the generation of the word *fois* in the lifeline of live words [*mots en vie*], of the words *vie* [life], *visa*, and *visit*, which will soon reappear in the same paragraph: as you know, *fois* comes from Latin *vicis*, which is not really a noun but first corresponds to a genitive form—in order to designate the turn, succession, the return, reciprocity, the alternative, therefore a certain replacement, a certain substitutive vicariousness. And one also finds *vicis* in Italian *vece*, in Spanish or in Portuguese, a language that, as you know, means a lot to her, in the form *vez*. "For the whole of life," for life, is irreplaceably the time, each time, in all the times. And what is necessary and impossible at the same time, necessary as impossible, in this thought of the "for the whole of life," is this logic of the "whole" as much as this logic of life. "Whole" does not so much signify the whole totality or totalization as the event of this "taking place," this substitution of the irreplaceable, this generative succession of the alliance or of "fiding [*fiance*]" in all the occurrences, all the times of the unique each time: here now, in the instant, on the spot, at this very moment for whoever gives themselves wholly to the moment [*sur l'heure pour qui se donne toute à l'heure*]. When it is "for life," "life" is the whole of life or nothing, and this "whole" in the whole of life derives as little from a logic of totality or of totalization as the "mighty power" of the "might" derives from a dynastic logic of power, of the possible or of potentiality, of the "I may" or "it is possible" of this potentate.

Where was I? Oh yes, the fish. Not the wish in "I wish I might" but the fish [*pas le "puissions" mais le poisson*]. Two words on "I never call out her name as I would toss a bit of fish." First, it is too easy to understand and I will not comment on the obvious: the name is not just a bit, first of all, although there are bits of names everywhere (*OR* for example); and to give is not to toss as one would a useful thing from a distance, without proximity and without extreme care. The name one gives, the name one calls, is not something one throws; it is an appellation of the unique in its entirety; and fish is cat food, etc.. One tosses it without throwing it. Two more words, though, talking of proper nouns, so I can ask myself how to avoid and why not avoid speaking here and there, in a cryptic or declared mode, about Hélène Cixous herself, in person, about her name, the one who signed *OR*, for example, which does not merge with the reciting subject in *OR*. This is a serious question and one every bit as unsolvable as to whether I should here address myself to her or not and whether I should or should not suspend what binds us in life at the moment when I am speaking about her writings. I do not want to call out her name as I would toss a bit of fish, but I will not decide, I will not decide once and for all and for all the times. I will improvise and leave you the responsibility to decide whether I am speaking of it/ her or not, whether I am addressing it/her or not, the work or life, the author or the one who says I, her fathers or her mother, etc..[84] You have to fill in the address; it is your address and your respon- sibility. Whether she is the one or the other, I hold that *her* work, *her* poetics of the event, *her* mighty power of nomination make all these undecidable distinctions tremble, in other words distinctions that are left more than ever to the most responsible, most inven- tive, and most irruptive decision, the only one that matters: the countersigning reading.

Where was I? Yes, the fish, two words about the name like a fish. Thessie, to whom, she says, "I never call out her name as I would toss a bit of fish," Thessie the real one, Thessie in flesh and blood arrived as *Messie* (fiction, 1996); she was thus admitted into the holy orders of literature as not one messiah could have been; but in so-called real life too, some of you here [*par ici*] can testify to that, she not only answers to her name, she also understands names and for example the word *crevette.*[85] Not only does one not call out her name as one would toss a prawn but one must know, as indeed I know, that the *crevette* she likes is a name that must not be pronounced in front of her. Because she hears, understands, and loves its vowels and consonants. She relishes the very name. There are names therefore that one must not pronounce in front of Thessie, outside certain times, if one does not want to arouse an insatiable desire in her. It is a whole culture of language and nomination for the lives of *all* living beings.

But since I am dealing with fish and names, with names of fish and seafood, with braids and nets of name, the oceanic mood I feel in front of this work is also reminiscent of what one feels about a miraculous catch. Magical, miraculous, and mystical: why? I ask myself why because, as a man of the Enlightenment, I would still like to give account and reason for this miraculous, mystical magic—which must not be an act of witchcraft. An inexhaustible magic, however. Why inexhaustible? Because, unlike what happens with Segalen and Térii the Reciter in *Les Immémoriaux*, there will never be a question of one day *neglecting* this braid, which is also a net of names. You know, after the passage I quoted a moment ago about the braid, which was called "Origin of the Word" for "it seemed to bring about speech," one could read this:

> Térii intended to neglect it soon: rehashed without respite, the con-secrated Sayings eventually followed from one another in his mouth, without error and effortlessly, just as the braided leaves that one casts adrift and hauls back, in armfuls, loaded with shimmering fish, follow one another in continuous lines.

One of the differences between her and this Reciter is that nothing can be allowed to be neglected or repeated one day, hence the infinity, quite simply because the shimmering fish are not caught by her net. The mighty fish are born from the *net* in which they are caught. That is what I call the poetics of the event. It produces magically, miraculously, and quasi-mystically the very thing it nominates. It brings about what it catches. That is why this omnipotent net draws away as much as draws back the living thing

that has stayed alive. How does it do that? How does it manage
to produce the thing by the grace of the nominal verb? Well, this
braided net, itself made of words, is also a net of telephone wires.
She makes the net of telephone wires. I will show it in a single
example, so as to recall at the same time what one must learn from
her, learn how to do, as I was saying, and learn from her what *to
do* means, and "how to do things with words,"[86] performatively do
things or events with words, by calling up names as one calls phone
numbers (for she also coined the phrase "to call up a name" [*faire
un nom*],[87] not to make a name for oneself [*se faire un nom*] but to
call up a name as one would call a phone number). The example
(among others, as always) comes from page 16 in *OR*, soon after
the now canonical page, "To reread, that is to say read, that is to
say resurrect-erase that is to say *forgetread* [oublire]."[88] The radio,
radiology, or radiotelephony—which outspeeds everything as it
"calls up the name"—are at work after one paragraph, one of those
songs "for life," one of these *Triumphs of Life*,[89] which also tell
of the exhaustion of the other, the breathlessness of the one who
complains that there is only one side—to the other side of which
one would sometimes like to pass. And to pass is also to pass to
the other side of life, to be passed by life and left aside, where there
are no more sides. Against the triumph of death and the hemorrhage of time, against the one in me who thinks of nothing else, it
is then enough to call and call up the name—not only to call the
number but also to call up the name. It is her order or command,
the mighty power of her command and of her telephone calling (I
will read this literally *radiant* song, this song of life resurrected at
her call, this song and effective charm, which is resurrected by the
call and by an enchantment—and you will see that the father and
the uncle are never far away: the radiophonology of Georges the
radiologist and the thoughtful humming of "my nuncle Freud"). It
is her command, it is also a genealogical order; it goes fast enough
to stop time at the moment when a phone call [*coup de téléphone*]
is made, in a moment, the trick of the phone call [*le coup* du *téléphone*]:

> At my command the hemorrhage of time stops and one single day

becomes two, and this same book that comes back (a)new already sixty times and not once read will come back to the call of its name. It is enough to call and the faraway, the forgotten or the dead one comes. How many a hundred years in a hundred years! And not only mine. Hundreds of others too.

In truth there are so many lives to be lived in life that often, too often, **we** can't any more [and after this **we**, the **you**, which follows a dash: a change of personal pronoun that would merit a pause that I cannot allow myself—JD]—tell the truth, it's too much, confess, you are the one who wishes life to end, how tiring to live living, this flaring up of every thought and nerve all day long is so exhausting. How often I have caught you brooding—you think nobody can see you?—how pleasant it will be to sleep at last. Those who live to the quick [*vivent au vif*] those who live living it is a furious effort, a rallying, astride on time, with sore buttocks bleeding hands, and with whipped breath.

[Here she begins a new paragraph and skips a line.—JD]

That's the trick of the phone call: I call the number and, by a magic that no amount of centuries will ever lessen, I catch you whether you are in Rome me in Berlin . . . [90]

You may have noticed how frequently she uses the word "catch" in her writing, but she always catches by a thread, a lock of hair, a writing line that fishes out, a funambulist's wire, a trapeze artist's net, or a telephone wire, even the lack of wire of a wireless, as one used to say when she was little, a wireless telegraphy, a radio, rays, a radiant radiology or radiotelephony.

. . . I catch you whether you are in Rome me in Berlin you in Santiago me in Recife I press a finger and my tongue against your ear my key in your heart.

What is distance? Two oceans under my forefinger. We are bodies in minds fast as the radio.

This "what is distance?" is an ontological question but also the dismissal of ontology, of the "what is?" What is distance? Implied: nothing when one is a telephone wizard, which is enough to cancel distance and the preliminary question of ontological knowledge, namely "what is distance?"

"What is distance? Two oceans under my forefinger. We are bodies in minds [*esprits*] fast as the radio."

In other words, *esprit* is not the mind in opposition to the body, on the other side of the body, and *esprit* is not the spirit, the *spiritus*, a breath that moreover would be fast, as if speed were a possible predicate of this entity [*étant*] that one calls *spiritus*, the breath in the telephone. No, the mind in which the body is, and not the body in general but the bodies we are, we who know how to phone (and not everybody is a telephone wizard; it is not enough to have a telephone), the mind in which we are bodies, it is not this or that which becomes fast here or there, like a pulse. No, or rather yes, the *spiritus*, the *pneuma* (and her father was the *pneuma* made man) is speed, the mind is this speed, it lives fast, it is therefore also technical, here telephonic, but its telephony did not wait for the invention of the telephone. For this telephony, which nonetheless also literally invented the telephone, is thought itself. The telephone is a poetico-technical invention, the *pneuma* is absolute speed in us, the speed of us, the radio that stops the hemorrhage of time. I myself should not have stopped the movement of this hymn. I resume.

> We are bodies in minds fast as the radio. Now I call up the name. Watch out!

This exclamation, "Watch out!" is extraordinary, truly magical, and it would merit centuries of analysis. Three lines earlier, there was the word "magic," you heard it, and the phrase "I call the number and, by a magic. . . . " Now [*or*] here she has just said: "Now I call up the name." She begins a new paragraph and exclaims or cries out: "Watch out!"

This warning, "Watch out!" is the conjurer's exclamation or injunction: address or skill, agility, dexterity, digital writing. On a stage, while the trapeze artist carries on with his acrobatic exercises, this magician talks to his public as he is about to pull his trick and conjure the thing out of himself, in a moment, right now [*tout à l'heure, tout de suite*], it is imminent, as if by an enchantment. Watch out, the impossible thing will take place under your eyes in a moment:

> Now I call up the name.
> Watch out!

Provided you watch carefully—but in any case you will not see a thing, since it goes so fast and the mighty power escapes you. Watch out for what you're going to see that you're going to see without seeing how it comes about, as if by an enchantment! "Now I call up the name," and where there is nobody, I have nothing in my hands, nothing in my pockets, the absent one is going to answer. To his name and for his name, which I give him or call up, like his number, he is going to answer—to his number: there will be a subscriber at the name and number I call. At the name I call up. As when I call the number—the number in a show, on a stage, by a magician or the phone number—these are all numbers. And she herself is quite a number, you're going to see. Then "Watch out!" means, first and foremost, watch carefully what I am doing around here as I am writing what you are reading here: around here I call up the name, for in writing I call up the name, and nothing else. Another monstration, another deictic of the conjurer who inconspicuously, discreetly, abstractedly shows you his finger with his finger, and what he has at the tips of his fingers. He also shows his address or his dexterity—on the text: read.

But to call up the name is to produce an appellation to which the other answers as much as oneself to transform into a name: I call up the name, watch out, and you're going to see my body, like that of an animal fanning its tail, mime and produce the name by becoming the name when on the spot I take the features of the name upon myself and in me. I call up the name, I call it, produce it, call upon it to answer, imitate it, and, always through substitution, metempsychotically become the name, like the number, I call and do a number [*je fais un numéro*], I am a number. In the series of substitutions. Of identity, sex, literary genre, and sexual *gender*. I am another "another" [*une autre "un autre"*], I am/follow it, hot on its trail and almost to the number, I give myself its surrogate name. All this by an enchantment, by the chant of an enchantment. I am/follow its name, I am/follow the name that I call up, etc.. I give it to myself, I add myself to it, I give myself over to it as if by an enchantment and like an animal performing a trick of magic at the magician's command. And you're going to see, once again the animal will soon appear suddenly, as early as the next line. Around here and everywhere.

Before continuing to read this passage, we should, if we had a few months at our disposal, summon all the telephones in her work (they are everywhere, like so many animals—a possible topic for six hundred dissertations—and a topic for a first question: are there more telephones or animals in the life and works of Hélène Cixous? Answer: animals are telephones and sometimes the other way around, and they multiply, in the prolifauny of all their animal, human, and divine metamorphoses. Besides "the dog is part of the telephone," as is said in the hymn to the telephone ("I will sing their telephone"). This hymn to the telephone rises, for example, in the heart of the sublime "Une Histoire idéale" in *Jours de l'an*, where, for Clarice, "It was on the phone that their books found their source. Unpublished source. Much purer source, Clarice would say, than her published books."[91]

The telephonic animals circulate between all the orders and all the rules, from the telephantasms and telefaun in *Anankè*, with its metaphones of phantomen [*fanthommes*], the "resistances of brotherly transferences [*transfrères*]," the sons or wires of the "little (t)elefaun [*petit éléfaune*]," its "introjection of the primal elefantasy"[92] and its "telephantasm of incorporation"[93] (the title of a chapter that names the "metonymic chains or the ones materialized in the guise of a wire, ribbons, locks [*mèches*], buckles, and other fastening devices . . . "[94] to the "cry of the telephone" and even to the critical moment of "teleaphony" in *La Fiancée juive—de la tentation*,[95] as critical a moment, it seems to me, as "The Betrayal" in *Beethoven*).[96]

Nothing would be more inane—but all the transferential resistance that is met by Hélène Cixous's work spins dizzily in these inanities—than to read these verbal and poetic inventions (telephantasms, for example) as simple puns she would have the knack for and which would come easily to her—or even as simple phantasms. Each time, what is at stake, in the production and according to the necessity (here the book is called *Anankè*) of a language event, is a *thoughtful analysis* of what binds and unbinds in the very living of the living [*le vivre même du vivant*], therefore in the animality of the animal, speed insofar as it cancels distance, the *tele* phenomenon, but at the same time binds and unbinds the appearing of the phenomenon, the *phainesthai*, insofar as it is indissociable from the *phantasma*, that is to say, both from the dream and the spectral phantom, of *revenance*, which *phantasma* also means. The exemplary privilege of the elephant, of this trope and of its trunk, is in the fact that it is both a living animal and bears in its name the root simulacrum of the very simulacrum, of the *phantasma*, of the seeming, and of the spectral, just as the privilege of the faun, as an animal or a Panic god, is in the fact that it binds free-floating desire, the satyr's ludic desire, to the speed of the telephonic voice. And that one must here analyze the phantasm as much as produce the event, in the same twofold gesture, is evidenced by the psychoanalytic code that she plays with and continually puts to work, as everywhere in *this* work, for example here with the "resistance of brotherly transference," the "introjection of the primal elefantasy," and the "telephantasm of incorporation." With the force of its forward thrust, its production of a living event, which it brings into the world and gives birth to, being delivered from it *while analyzing it*, this analytic power charges up the whole work. In *Anankè* (1979), while we are on the subject, the last chapter, the green chapter (each chapter is named after a color), is called "To Make the Child and to Interpret It." It features a prodigious delivery scene, which carries and also gives birth to this theory according to which there are always two moments (and I believe them to be inseparable around here): "To make the child and to interpret it." She writes: "There are two moments: to make the child and to interpret it." Further on, still in italics, someone speaks: "—*There are two times: a time to make love and a time to analyze it.*" To make and to interpret, indissociably, but also to make and to interpret interpretation, for example to "do psychoanalysis," as the phrase goes, to make an analysis, which she does all the time, and interpret psychoanalysis, for example all the discourses of Uncle Freud, who is always there, in a corner, on his couch, or on the line in the next room [*à côté*], like an answering machine questioned by the prodigal niece.

Let us leave Freud on the line, we will come back to him in a moment, let us make him wait a bit, just long enough for us, around here, to draw a line of conduct and a line of reading: namely that there is no rule for reading the prodigies of this mighty power, there is no other rule than to invent the rule with each letter in order to countersign, to grant oneself the inspired verve of this "might [*puisse*]" (the magnitude of this "might of the may"), to accord/agree *with it while subjunctivating for ourselves* everything it says or while subjunctivating to it, all(o)ying oneself to it according to the alliance or the alloy, that is to say, at once to make and to interpret while countersigning. If interpretation supposes analysis, that is to say, the *analuein* of the unbinding that unties, then *to make* or *do*, on the contrary, comes down to binding, to binding oneself and allying oneself [*à se lier et à s'allier*], to doing the contrary at the same time. Only an act of writing as an act of love that binds and *reads* [*lie et* lise]—*might* read as it unbinds the threads, while weaving an alliance in the analysis of unbinding itself—can measure up to this text for the invention of a criticism as a poetics of reading. As I was preparing for this session, I prowled a lot around the relationships between subjunctivity and subjectivity, these two moods or modes of subjugation, subjection, and subordination. I did so with the intention of proving that the apparently subordinated might of the subjunctive was potentially mightier [*en puissance plus puissante*], from a performative point of view, than that of the present indicative of the verb, therefore of the constative, for example, of the verb "to be" in the *this is,* the "it is" of ontology, and therefore the ontological idea of subjectivity or objectivity. For "might" is the absolute performative. Any performative, any phantasmatic omnipotence of the performative draws from the mighty power of this "might." Only an affection, the affective part of an event, can remind it of its limit. The subjunctive is mightier, from the subordinate clause, than the ontological main clause. The ontological main clause is this "this is [*c'est*]" cut short by the hatchet [*hache*] of H.C. H.C. is something other than the "it is [*c'est*]" of the ontological main clause. Provoked into interesting myself in this subjunctive modality in a way I had never done before, I wished to be quite clear in my own mind: I looked up the word "subjunctive" in my dictionary and I immediately fell upon this: "The subjunctive is mainly the mood of the subordinate clause. First example: 'That Jacques be alive did not surprise her much'" (Roger Martin du Gard).

Uncle Freud is still waiting on the line. For example, again he is not far off when, in *Jours de l'an*, the telephone comes into the same configuration with the two sides, the right and the left, speed, the spirit of inspiration and the order given—and you are at last going to hear the *par ici*:

> . . . it's to the right, it's to the left, a little clearer, a little faster, this way [*par ici*]. [New paragraph.—JD]
> In the meantime, I went on ahead. I have an inspiration? I follow her. She moves faster than we do. "Come on!" That's an order. Coming from my most imperious life . . . [97]

Further on, on the other page, these two words appear: "the telephone," both on their own, on a single line. In the same movement, still further, she is on the telephone [*parle au téléphone*]. But she does not speak *on the telephone*, as one says *to speak on the telephone*. No, she really speaks *to* the telephone; she speaks in its direction [*à son adresse*], addresses it and says: "O telephone. . . . " She even asks it for forgiveness, for "telephone" not only represents an animal life, even when there is an answering machine; telephone is somebody who must forgive her when she asks him to let her sleep, not to ring anymore. And we will see later why this is no zoo-anthropomorphic animism. Two pages further, she forgives herself after accusing herself, equally blithely: of being sad being happy, and of dreaming. "If I must accuse myself, it's of committing dreams."

Let us now come back to where the magician who *calls up the name* as if by an enchantment has just said to us "Watch out":

> Now I call up the name.
> Watch out!
>
> [A big blank space of waiting, then a date, and here is the animal that had been announced.—JD]
>
> 6 December 1936
> (*Enter my uncle Freud*).
>
> . . . Here is the reason why one can love an animal: (beyond all the differences of organic development) we are next of kin by the same enchantment. I am really talking about the enchanting chant, this un-limited sentenceless willful language comparable to God's unknown language. So my uncle Freud thought.
> "That's why often, while caressing Jofi, I caught myself humming a melody that I know well although I am no musician . . . "

The musician of this *enchanting chant*—the musician that the subject of utterance says he is not, although he is humming, as Freud would hum—is a *male* musician. Not a female musician. We would have—a truly infinite work—to deal with the truth of the sex of this masculine, like that of the author who is the daughter of the dead-fathers, as with the trouble, the instability, the infinitely intertwined, criss-cross multiplicity of the sexual identities that share the signature of this work, replacing one another anywhere with unspeakable craft, tricks, and subtleties—making all the more difficult or improbable a reading that would not make the same expenditure—and with reading comes the political strategy that would instrumentalize this enchanting chant like a feminist theorem or a philosophical thesis.

That I would have the time to deal with it is rather unlikely. But one will not unbind the mighty power of the enchanting chant [*puissance de l'enchant*], in its tongues, from the powers of sexual difference, which, as a difference, but from both sides of the difference, is at work in *this* work as, to my knowledge, in none other, in no other work: the differential of might itself. At most, im-potency faced with the very event, and its affect. Beyond any performative.

Seven years before *OR*, in *Jours de l'an* (1990), another scene of the "Now I am going. . . . Watch out!" announced, like a number, the imminence of the stroke of the magic wand, the performative operation whose technique will in a moment, on the spot [*tout à l'heure, sur l'heure*], without delay, straightaway, like a *fiat*, make light and conjure up a character created, as in Genesis or in science fiction, from nearly nothing, almost ex nihilo. I say "science fiction" because, with all these telephones and this high-tech feel, her magic is also ahead of its times and connives with cyberliterature, with its heroic specters or its virtual idols. At the top of a page that will remain blank, one could already read in *Jours de l'an*:

> Watch out, because the hour is going to sound. In three lines. I collect myself one last time. As before a separation. Now I am going to open the door. Now I am going to turn on the light. And you will see. I turn it on: . . . [98]

After this colon, it is like the raising of the curtain in a theater, a big blank page, and the play begins on the other side, on the other page. The character is simply called death, "my death," "thy death," "your death." I leave you with them. "Death [says the author of the play—JD] is not what we think. Often it is alive, whereas we only think of it as dead."

Since we will come back in a moment, while still at the time of *OR*, to the question of a certain omnipotence, I should therefore myself like to think, and above all make you think, a mighty power, that of Hélène Cixous, hers, the one she testifies to and the one she experiments with. Everywhere she *assays* a mighty power of the "might," which might have nothing to do any longer with the possible and with power. It would at least be older and younger than them, taking them and taking itself beyond the possible, beyond power, and their dynasty. As if this omnipotence were in league with the im-possible. It would do the impossible. It would therefore attest to unpower, as well as to vulnerability and death—hence the magic of what, by a stroke of writing, does the impossible.

"Magic"—now, that is a tempting word, a dangerous temptation to name this omnipotence. What would be at stake here, in-
voking the magical invocation, is not to describe a phantasm of
animist and infantile omnipotence, nor occult incantations taken
seriously by an obscurantist knowledge. On the contrary, a certain
exploration, both theoretical and practical, of the letter, the *tekhnè*
of a certain pragmatic, the performative force of the writing that
we salute here, all this would be used as an experimental analyzer
for the irrecusable effectiveness of such *phantasmata*, a Greek word
thanks to which one would refer here to phantasms as well as to
dreams and their revenants, in accordance with the very usage of
this term. It would then be the place of one of these confronta-
tions with Freud, of which I can only indicate the necessity yet
again as I am renouncing it.

Turned toward Uncle Freud, we could have sought to make
things a little more complicated for him by putting this forward:
so that might *might* make something come as much as it *might,*
is it not necessary, in the very agency of this mighty power of the
"*might*" [*du* "puisse" *ou de la* "puisse"], there where it takes its place,
for desire to be able to reach where the distinction between phantasm and the so-called actual or external reality does not yet take
place and has no place to be? Not that this distinction is thereby
discredited, far from it, but one would have to rethink it from this
place where it does not yet take place. To take this one example:
in this place, where the mighty power of the "might" announces
itself, the border would not yet be secured between real seduction
and the phantasm of seduction, this historical crux of Freudian
psychoanalysis. Where phantasmatic seduction does not work, it
is because it is not powerful enough, the law of might being auto-
immune, grappling with the impossible, which singularly compli-
cates matters.

But it is not the X-ray of that particular Freud which seems to
me the most urgently called for. It would be rather the X-ray of
the Freud who, for example in *Totem and Taboo*, devotes at least
one chapter to "Animism, Magic, the Omnipotence of Thoughts."
This is the title of chapter 3: "*Animismus, Magie und Allmacht der*

Gedanken." More precisely, in this chapter, I would quickly x-ray three organic articulations only in order to point out their problematic snags or their opaque spots, that is to say, the very thing that is not self-evident and can be puzzling, thus marking the limit of Freudian analysis, as well as, simultaneously, what in it remains to come—and which I read in the mighty power put to work and signed by the hand of Freud's niece by marriage. In *Totem and Taboo*, he had thus admitted owing the phrase "omnipotence of thoughts (*Allmacht der Gedanken*)" to one of his very intelligent patients. The Rat Man—for he is the one—was confiding his experiences of omnipotence to him: he only had to think about a person in order to come across him or her, not to mention the telepathic bonds with the living, the dead, and the dying properly speaking. In *The Rat Man*, which Freud's niece knows probably better than anybody else, the analysis of this feeling of omnipotence begins on the same page as this note—which I thought I had to speak ill of elsewhere—on the alleged superiority of patriarchy, which appeals to reason, paternity being a fabrication of judgment (*a legal fiction*, as Stephen said in *Ulysses*),[99] whereas, on the side of my living mother, I know perceptibly and without a doubt that she is and who she is. Let's leave it at that; that was said elsewhere. It is in the vicinity of psychoanalytic naïveté, the most widely shared thing in the world and in history,[100] that Freud proposes to analyze his patient's feeling of omnipotence. Although I am not able to x-ray his analysis here, I laser in on those moments that would merit a prolonged observation around here. One of these passages has to do with the father's death, which is said to have played a determining role for the Rat Man, all of whose obsessions tend to make up not for the father's death but for parricidal wishes, so much so that whenever he said "beyond," *jenseits*, in other words, "on the other side," Freud authorized himself to translate as, I quote: "If my father was still alive." And *The Rat Man* is nothing but a long development insisting on the fact that love does not extinguish hatred, quite the contrary, nor the care for life the death wish: *for life* would be around here at the service of *for death*. In the same patient, according to the same logic, the one that would bring about the infantile megalomania of the omnipotence of thought, Uncle Freud believes he can detect an unresolved conflict, namely the normal oscillation between man and woman as objects of love. It is the conflict in front of which, he says, one places the child by asking the famous question: "Who do you love best, Mummy or Daddy?" The oscillation then stays with him all life long, despite individual differences in the evolution of affective intensities and in the fixation of final sexual goals. But normally this opposition soon loses the aspect of a neutral contradiction. It is no longer an inexorable alternative. A margin is created in order to satisfy the unequal demands of the two parties, the mother and the father, although in the normal man himself the depreciation of persons of a given sex always goes together with a proportionately higher esteem for persons of the opposite sex. We briefly saw how the question "Who do you love best, Mummy or Daddy?" was dealt with, dealt with again by her, not far from the *Introduction to Narcissism,* as well as the question "Your dead father, would you like it if he wasn't?" whose answer "I cannot look . . . in the face." But let's leave that aside; I had announced *three* problematic *snags* and three opaque areas in the Freudian analysis of the "omnipotence of thoughts."

A. The first snag that crops up, in *Totem and Taboo,* is the moment when Freud feels obliged to grant an exceptional privilege to art. Freud acknowledges that art would be the only domain in which, in the advanced phase of human civilization that is ours, the omnipotence of thoughts (*Allmacht der Gedanken*) continues to be exercised. It has been kept up (*erhalten geblieben*) to this very day. One is right to compare the artist to a magician (*Zauberer*), he says, and to speak of art's magic (*Zauber der Kunst*). Before that, Freud had distinguished several phases in the psychical development of humankind: an *animist* phase, which, as far as chronology and contents are concerned, would correspond to a "narcissism" or to an infantile megalomania, then a *religious* phase, which would correspond to the object choice (*Objektfindung*) and would be characterized by the child's attachment to its parents, and last the *scientific* phase, the phase of "knowledge" (*wissenschaftliche Phase*).

It is then maturity, the time when one gives up the pleasure principle, adjusts to the object's reality in the external world, from the
point of view of reason, of (especially psychoanalytic) science and
philosophy. In this last phase, one would give up the animist or
religious omnipotence of thought, one would resign oneself to
death. One would acknowledge it.

Without so much as smiling at such evolutionist scientism,
which is at once coarse, dated, but also full of indisputable common sense, one may wonder what this exception of art as magic
means. Why did art not disappear, if it still survives? And why
must Freud hesitate to turn art's magic into a mere animist remnant, the residue of a "narcissism"? Why does he draw back from
this issue of art? There are at least two signs that testify to this
failure: *on the one hand*, the inability to account for the residual
persistence of what would only be a remnant and a survival in
this evolutionism; *on the other hand*, an utterly insufficient and
inconsistent, traditional concept of art, which would be at once
an "illusion" (it is Freud's word: an "illusion" that produces effects of the affect [*Affektwirkungen*] "as if it were something real"
["*als wäre es etwas Reales*"]) and, as an illusion, purely and simply
a representational and reproductive mimicry. This clearly appears
in the long embarrassed note devoted to Reinach's book, *L'Art et
la magie*, in which art is considered solely in its representational,
mimetic, illusion-producing form (from the so-called primitive
painters onward, who left on the cave walls representations of
beasts of prey that they feared or wanted to exorcize, etc.).[101] If,
as Freud says, art was originally something other than "art for art's
sake" but first served tendencies toward magical efficacy that are
extinct today, why would he persevere? Anyway, who said that art
had to be essentially "art for art's sake"? Moreover, Freud acts as
if, first of all, "effects of the affect" were not real events, as if the
"as if" had no real effect. What Freud seems strangely ignorant
of, which comes down to misunderstanding nonrepresentational
art—or nonconstative art, productive art, the poietic dimension
of art—is the knowledge and power of language in general, in the
order of psychoanalysis in particular, on the side of the analyst and

of the analysand, of theory, practice, and the analytic institution, where performative power acts and produces always according to ways that are at once rational, technical, *and magical.* The effect, both affective and effective, of a performative is always magical in appearance. It always operates as if by an enchantment. In practice and in theory, in technique—in particular, that of psychoanalysis. Who better than Freud himself at once showed it, illustrated it, and ignored it? I think that, on this point as well as on others, it is always by recalling him to himself that his niece could ruthlessly criticize and mock him.

B. Second snag. There is something more interesting in Freud's half-baked theory about the omnipotence of thoughts (at least in *Totem and Taboo,* for what he senses in his texts on telepathy would be more troubled, more troubling, more daring). Whereas he has just reduced the phantasm of the omnipotence of thoughts to narcissism, to infantile megalomania, to animism and its technique, magic (*Die Technik des Animismus, die Magie,* he says), Freud thinks it necessary to specify that the presuppositions (*Voraussetzungen*) of magic are more originary and more ancient (*ursprünglicher und älter*) than the doctrine of spirits (the theory of ghosts: *Geisterlehre*), which forms the kernel of animism. There would therefore be a pre-animism. Freud then evokes the theory and the book by Marett, *Pre-animistic Religion,* and proposes to call it "animatism" (*Animatismus*). This animatism is not a mere belief in the spirits of the dead. It is something like a theory of living, of being-alive, of livingness [*vivance*],[102] of universal being-for-life (*Lehre von der allgemeinen Belebtheit*), which Jankélévitch senior somewhat excessively translates as "universal hylozoism," referring to the doctrine that lends life, *zoe,* to everything, in particular to so-called inorganic, dead matter (*hyle*), so that everything would be life, including the apparent nonlife of matter deprived of breath. Freud does not quite say this, even though what he suggests more or less comes down to the same thing: the *Belebtheit* of livingness [*vivance*] or of liveliness [*vivacité*], the live-ance of being in life [*le* vivement *de l'être en vie*] ("I live. . . . I am the place

of revival," she says),[103] this reviviscence of life would be the element, the only one, a universal element, since it has no limits or
no other side: there is no side for nonlife. Now what does Freud
say about the pre-animistic or "animatistic" experience of this universal *Belebtheit* deprived of another side? What does he say about
the experience of this *Belebtheit*, which is not life in inanimate
things but the always living experience of all that enters the field
of this life? What does he say about the experience, which can
only encounter the life that it is, that it lives, its life, even when it
has to do with the nonliving, when an eschatology is announced,
an experience of the extreme last, of the last extremity, for which
the death drive itself would be *for life*? And even the tendency
toward nirvana? What does he, Freud, say about this animatistic
pre-animism? Well, nothing. He says there is nothing to say, or
that there is very little to say about this pre-animism, almost nothing else (*wenig mehr*), at least from experience (*aus der Erfahrung*,
a point forgotten by the French translation). What experience is
he speaking of? It is very simple in his mind: of anthropo-ethno-
logical experience. One has yet to encounter a people lacking any
representation of spirits (*Geistervorstellung*), that is to say, a people
that has not determined pre-animism or animatism as religious
animism. This remark is interesting for what it says and what it
does not say. It says or implies that any people, as a people, any
culture known and determined by experience, has its own *Geistervorstellung*, a theory of revenants, and determines itself as the culture of a people as it determines an originary *Belebtheit* and gives
it a specific figure, that is to say as it populates and populates itself
with spectral representations: there is no culture without *unheim-
lich* spectrality, without an organization of haunting. It is very interesting and fruitful, but what Freud does not say as he says that
is what this universal *Belebtheit*—which is not yet culturally determined as an animism, which, unlike animism, is not yet about to
become, or is not already, a religion of the dead in their surviving
ghosts—can be, will have been, could have been, in potentiality
[*en puissance*]; a *Belebtheit* of which we can say nothing by anthro-
pological, culturalist, or ethnological experience, and which is not

even a philosophical doctrine (as is hylozoism, which the French translation talks about), but a quasi-originary *Belebtheit* that must, if not present itself, at least announce itself to some pre-empirical or pre-positive experience.

Well, it is this experience that, according to me, writes and analyzes itself, maybe *experiments itself,* one should say, each time that in the life and works of Hélène Cixous the mighty power of the "might" is at work, that is to say is being tested, as a work of life, as living, or, subjunctively, as "oh, that life be lived, for life [*vivement le vivre, pour la vie*]." Experience means the performativity of a writing that travels and crosses the continental distances at full speed and on all possible rhythms (which "experience" or "experimentation" or even "expertise," or *Erfahrung,* means). This signed experience does what it says; it puts this *Belebtheit* to work and to the test, tries it out: to see, out of a living desire and an experimental curiosity, by provoking the event, by making-letting it happen, before any philosophical, scientific, or cultural thesis on being as life or on the essence of the living. It is not an ontology of life (for example, in the sense of the huge debate between Heidegger and all the philosophies of life and, even more, all the biologisms). This experience of *Belebtheit,* which makes and analyzes the phantasm, which makes and analyzes birth, is not a position on the essence of being as life. The life of this *Belebtheit* is not, it is not an "entity [*étant*]"; it is a mighty power of the "might" without another side, without a contrary. Death is neither unknown nor denied nor avoided; it represents a great character of this literature, but it is simply not a contrary and another opposite side of living, a yonder or a beyond.

This being said, and signed, in (the) place of what Uncle Freud leaves unsaid, but not against him. For in a way the deployment of this poetico-performative, magical might does have to do with the most originary narcissism that Freud thinks he can recognize at the origin of the "omnipotence of thoughts." The omnipotence of thought is narcissistic, it is this tautology of absolute speed we were talking about, the econo-meto-homonymy of living life, which, a moment ago, could only say "me," "mine"—but one should not get carried away with speed and hasten to believe one knows what narcissism is and means. Narcissism has no contrary, no other side, no beyond, and love for the other, respect for the other, self-denial in favor of the other do not interrupt any narcissistic movement. *Belebtheit* is narcissistic, life lets itself be lived and outlived in accordance with originary narcissism. One must love oneself living in order to love the other. Only the impotence of a petty narcissism blocks off love for the other. This is, as you know, what Echo teaches Narcissus through an effect of language, almost a play on words, in the *Metamorphoses* (" '*Ecquis adest?' et 'adest' responderat Echo . . .* "; " *. . . voce 'veni!' magna clamat: vocat illa vocantem*").[104] To love the other as oneself supposes the teletachycardic unlimitedness of narcissistic might. The mightier narcissism is, the more it loves the other. And in order to love the other as oneself more than oneself (introjection and incorporation), this surplus of might is needed, always more of it, this more than possible that is the most impossible. (Here, as Angelius Silesius says, *das Überunmöglichste ist möglich*, which can be translated in two different ways: either the most impossible is possible, or else the *more than* impossible is possible; it all depends on the stroke of genius and how good it is at making excess, *über*, tremble between the comparative and the superlative, or else at declining the superlative on the side of a certain subjunctive.) Narcissism is the elementary condition for love. Apart from myself, will I dare say that I know nobody who is more impossibly narcissistic than Hélène Cixous, in her-life-her-works? I could say that, apart from myself. That's why she and I keep each other at a respectful distance, and with the greatest possible respect, each to one side. "That, to my knowledge, nobody might be more narcissistic than me," as I have therefore just said, apart from myself, I could prove that this is a necessarily universalizable maxim for whoever knows what to orient oneself in thought means—or simply to orient oneself, from one side to the other, from the always subjective difference of the right hand and of the left hand: *on the one hand, on the other hand.* Like the French grammar of such an undecidably autobiographical sentence as "I write (to) myself [*je*

m'écris]" or "We write ourselves / each other [*nous nous écrivons*]"
all the time. But let's leave it at that; that would still be like talking about oneself.

The work and thought of H.C. are and are not a hylozoism, and
the omnipotence of thoughts (*Allmacht der Gedanken*) at work in
what she writes is nothing but a modest, loving thought of what
the subjunctivity of omnipotence might be. Call that desire, the
sublimated beauty of desire or the desire of sublime beauty if you
like. Narcissus or Echo.

C. The third snag, the third problematic task in this passage
from *Totem and Taboo*, brings us back again to her, to her work.
Scarcely further, after he has just fallen silent about the pre-animism of *Belebtheit*, Freud narrates something like the arrival of
the side, that is to say, of the limit that, in the sacrifice and acknowledgment of death, puts a stop to narcissism and death, but
precisely where there is no limit or other side. He calls that "necessity," in Greek, *Anankè*. Now, in the movement he thus analyzes, what seems to me to be most original here, and for us most
striking and most necessary, precisely, is that he allows a double,
apparently contradictory or undecidable gesture: to know and acknowledge [*connaître et reconnaître*] *Anankè*, that is to say death, is
to deny it at the same time. At the same time, in the same movement, on the spot [*sur l'heure*]. To acknowledge is to deny [*dénier*]
or to renege [*renier*]. To acknowledge is not to acknowledge. Conversely, not to acknowledge, to deny, to renege, is to acknowledge,
I will say *de-negate* [de-renier]. In the enigma of this acceptance of
death, of this knowledge that acknowledges (*Anerkennung*) death,
but of this re-cognizing knowledge [*connaissance re-connaissante*] *as*
negation and of this negation *as* denial [*dénégation*], *Verleugnen*, in
this acknowledgment that denies and misunderstands [*méconnaît*]
what it knows and re-cognizes [*re-connaît*], well, this is where the
side, the other side of the life without sides, precisely takes itself
away. One should then think denial [*dénégation*], which to this
day remains unthought in that respect, from *Anankè* and from the
gesture of the body that surrenders to *Anankè*. Such is the one and

double gesture (*mit derselben Geste*, says Freud), such is the *gestus* that must be made and interpreted—and *gesture* is a very powerful, very rich word, which seems to me appropriate here for the theatrical, generative, and performative scope of the writing of the body we are talking about, I'll come back to that straightaway. Let us listen to Freud speaking about this "same gesture" (*mit derselben Geste*):

> . . . man's first theoretical achievement (*die erste theoretische Leistung des Menschen*)—the creation of spirits (*die Schöpfung der Geister*) . . .

Freud uses two different words, *Leistung* and *Schöpfung*, to indicate clearly that this theory has been a productive and constitutive operation, *Leistung*, as an ex nihilo creation, *Schöpfung*, which can equally be an artistic creation: phantoms are creatures of men and of works of art, and these creations are theoretical by themselves. The production of the spectral is theoretic, the phantasmal or phantasmatic visions are theorems and theatrical theorems.

> Thus man's first theoretical achievement (*die erste theoretische Leistung des Menschen*)—the creation of spirits (*die Schöpfung der Geister*)—seems to have arisen from the same source (*aus derselben Quelle*) as the first moral restrictions [*sittlichen Beschränkungen*: the source of creation is thus a limitation, a border—JD] to which he was subjected [*er sich unterwirft*: literally subjects himself, subjectivates himself, subserves to—JD]—the observances of taboo [*die Tabuvorschriften*: the prescriptive or prohibitive writings of the prohibiting law: creation creates the revenant and phantasmatic theory by subscribing, by subordinating itself to its own limiting prescription—JD]. The fact that they have the same origin (*Gleichheit des Ursprungs*) need not imply, however, that they arose simultaneously [*Gleichzeitigkeit der Entstehung*: therefore, from the same birthplace they do not become established or do not emerge at the same time—hence what is called history, all the histories of morality, religion, science and technique, etc.—JD]. If the survivors' position in relation to the dead was really what first caused primitive man to reflect and compelled him to hand over some of his freedom of action, then these cultural products would constitute a first acknowledgment (*Anerkennung*) of Aναvκη,

which opposes human narcissism [which is opposed to it, which thwarts it, *widersetzt*—JD]. Primitive man would thus be submitting to the supremacy of death [the superior might of death: *Übermacht des Todes*—JD] with the same gesture (*mit derselben Geste*) with which he seemed to be denying it (*durch die er diesen zu verleugnen scheint*).[105]

The following sentence begins: "If we had the courage to continue. . . . "[106]

Freud did not say that this gesture consists in acknowledging and denying *at the same time*, but that the acknowledgment of *Anankè*, of what is effective, takes place in the same gesture through which the first man seems to deny it. He does not deny, since he acknowledges, but he seems to deny; it is *as if* he denied what he acknowledges. This same gesture comes to the same thing without doing so, and it is in the direction of this "as if" that we should have the courage to continue. It is, for example, the courage of this immense, thoughtful poem called *Anankè*, whose richness so overwhelms me that I hardly dare touch on it. Besides, *Anankè* names the courage, in a place where we find again Thessie and Molly's "yes I will yes." The double affirmation of this "yes" is at once courage itself and the first name of love:

> "*Do you have the courage?*" my friend said, and straightaway I said "*yes*," and the first name of love was: "*Yes I will yes.*" Do it . . .
> [Would that you might what follows, at least until:—JD]
> I had the courage but I felt apprehensive, such an event only happens once.[107]

Courage is not the opposite of fear, and *Anankè* deals with, and weaves together, all these questions: courage is the courage of what she also calls "the question," that of the "most real name of my Necessity," and "the question" is Eve. *Anankè* puts into play and on stage again all the elephantasms of incorporation and introjection, and especially Narcissus—not only from *Zur Einführung des Narzissmus*, called by its name in *Les Commencements* at the moment of the aforesaid "first question" ("Who do you love best, Mummy or Daddy?"),[108] but Narcissus himself, of whom it is said that one must (it is a subtitle) "fight against Narcissus with seven fears." A subchapter that opens with a scene in which recognition *as* avoidance, avoidance *in* recognition (what takes place around here again, after all), are named by their names at the arrival of narcissus (with a small letter, like the flower):

> "*This is why you recognize him*"—always avoided—the pursuer, "*nothing in the world could have avoided him*" . . . it was narcissus, no doubt, and I couldn't place him . . . I couldn't recognize myself.[109]

But one must read everything, of course, letter by letter: I ill-treat everything by thus selecting and chopping with unforgivable violence. Unable to do justice to this book, as to the other fifty in fact, in such conditions I merely underline something of what I decided a moment ago to name her *gesture* and her *experience*, a double and coordinated gesture, capable of doing things with words, of carrying with a gestion that is also a gestation and a birth: *gestio* means to be carried away with desire, to burn with desire, and *gesto* means to carry, and *gestari* to be carried, to travel; and her experilous, experimental experience, the dangerous journey (*Gefahr, Fahren*), the expert crossing of her experience (*Erfahrung*), her experimentation, her test of originary *Belebtheit*, are gestures and an experience, operations and an opus, a putting to work, which hold together and are held by the tight dovetailing of experimental technique (always a bit ironic: one must do it just to see, to try it out) and of magic, knowledge, know-how, and enchantment, at the point where, for the oppositionless narcissism of *Belebtheit*, there is no longer any contradiction between the experience of magic and the experimentation of the most objective techno-science. For example, all the experiences or experiments of the telephone and of telepathy are at once magical and purely technical, even cybernetic and transgenic. Her work would be transgenic at the point where, beyond genres, it crosses genealogies in order to produce new bodies, but also because it does so according to the mighty power of a language that stretches beyond the naturalness of the genetic, beyond the calculable program of a genome. In this place, from which her work springs, and to which it points [*où point son oeuvre, et qu'elle pointe*], the alleged disenchantment of the world (*Entzauberung der Welt*), which has been dinned into our ears since Max Weber[110] and which opposes magic to technique, may no doubt have a lot of sense and pertinence up to this point but it loses any pointed relevance. Like the opposition between faith and knowledge. And the point where this opposition appears, can be thought, determined—and annulled—is the point where she enchants technique that has remained technique, where she thinks and writes. No distinction then can hold any longer between magic and technique, faith and knowledge, and so on. The one and the other are *might*, I am not saying they are *capable* of might but I'd like to say, I wish that they *might* might [puissent *la puissance*]. Even before having to decide between phantasms of the omnipotence of thought and an effective might, it would have been necessary to think might itself, both the might of thought and the thought of might, the thinking of thought as might. This takes place before and so that the phantasm goes out and meets [*à la rencontre de*] the other, an other of the phantasm that is always fortuitous [*de rencontre*], met by chance [*croisé*] rather than commanded, rather than *ordered*, by appointment.

That's what happens around here. As we will verify, what happens here, in the gest of this experience, is not something else or the opposite of the impossible or, if you prefer, of impotence. This remains a thought of the Enlightenment beyond the Enlightenment. That's why, in spite of all the magic, the enchanting chant, and the charm of this experience, I never have the feeling, on my side at least, of any morbid witchcraft, any obscurantist or occult thaumaturgy, nor any irrational bewitchment [*envoûtement*]. Even the word *envoûtement*, when she uses it, and if you really read her, does not simply mean "bewitchment." For example, in the chapter from *Messie* entitled "États d'août," the word *envoûtement* is only one of the musical measures in a symphony in *out* (*toute* [all], *toujours* [always], *au mois d'août* [in the month of August], *doute* [doubt], *doutaient* [doubted], *redouter* [redoubt], *elle doutait de son doute* [she doubted her doubt]): the bewitchment is also the bewitching return, every year, of these syllables, me [*le moi*], and the month [*mois*] of August.

Here, for another beginning, I would have given anamnesis, as the anamorphosis of a great poem, a chance. During a recollection, I would have resurrected, under features that would have left it both similar and unrecognizable, Gorgias' hymn to Helen. Not Saint Georges's but Gorgias'. I would have reinterpreted what, in this encomium of Helen, Gorgias says about the power of persuasion of the *logoi*, of speech as might (speech is a great dynast, he says: *logos dunastes megas estin*). Gorgias cautions us especially against diverting this might into witchcraft magic:

> God-inspired enchantments (*ai gar entheoi dia logôn epôidai*) through speeches induce pleasure and reduce sorrow. By intercourse with the soul's belief, the mighty power of the enchantment (*e dunamis tes epôides*) seduces and persuades her and moves by sorcery [*fascination*]. Two arts of sorcery and magic (*goeteias de kai mageias dissai tekhnai*) have been discovered; they are deviations of the soul and deceptions of belief. . . . So what reason is there against Helen having been surprised by a charm (a song, a hymn, *umnos*, an incantation)?[111]

Further, evoking the mighty power of discourse (*tou logou dunamis*) again, he denounces those words that, between the different, beneficial or evil, species of *pharmakon*, sometimes act as bad pharmaceutical substances, adulterate and bewitch the soul (*psukhèn epharmakeusan kai exegoeteusan*). But I would have registered in my anamorphosis that this perversion, this corruptibility must always remain possible in order to allow benediction to run its course.

Since we are in Troy and my palinode begins an encomium of *Hélène* once again, yet as if it were for the first time, it is perhaps the place to recall Stesichorus' palinode here. Plato recalls it in the *Phaedrus* (243 a b). Like Homer, Stesichorus (first half of the sixth century) had spoken ill of Helen. In short, he had reproached her with her art of substitution: she was supposed to have indulged in multiple loves and marriages. Stesichorus had lied and he became blind. But since he was cultivated and a *mousikos* (learned, a poet and a familiar of the Muses), he confessed his fault and composed a *palinodia*, that is to say, a song in a different key to mean also a recantation through which one goes right back, goes back over what one has said, goes back in the opposite sense but also by beginning again with the beginning, which *palin* means, one picks up again right from the beginning, at the point when one nearly lied or betrayed. As soon as he had thus sung this palinode, Stesichorus recovered his eyesight. In his palinode, his recantation, the one by which he acknowledged and confessed his mistake, one could hear the sound of these words:

> *ouk est'etumos logos outios*
> *oud'ebas en neusin euselmois*
> *oud ikeo pergama Troias*

> There is no truth in this language (this language is not *etumos*: true, proper, appropriate—he has lied)
> No, thou didst not step onto the well-decked vessels
> No, thou didst not come to the castle of Troy!

As he was recanting, Stesichorus saw fit to add that it was not Helen but her ghost, Helen's ghost (*Elenès eidôlon*), who followed Paris to Troy and for whom the madmen fought in Troy. (Plato makes it clear in the *Republic* IX, 586 c, on the occasion of a discourse on the idol, on the *eidolon* as ghost, specter, or revenant.)

You may still remember that, in one of my earlier beginnings, while quoting from *OR*, we had just heard about life and might, just as omnipotence will be at issue in a moment:

> These are lives of power, at great depths, unsubjected to the clock . . .

Now [*or*] you know that *OR* is also an extraordinary symphony of the clock, on all the things named or signifying the clock, on the theme of such and such a specific clock in the town of Oran, and all the chance felicities [*heurs et bonheurs*] of the signifier *or*, in the heart of a father's earth and georgic name, but also, that way, the delicate work of a watchmaker goldsmith, which would

require centuries of deciphering through the homonymic, dissyn-
onymic, and synonymic mechanism of the letter.

> These are lives of power, at great depths, unsubjected to the clock,
> which hang by a thread, like all lives of this kind. Apparently a great
> sobriety but, on the contrary, in the body and in the head, an iron
> constitution is needed to bear the fleeting touch of eternity violently
> brushing against you.[112]

This "fleeting touch of eternity" is an anticipation or a recall:
the experience of eternity is in no way foreign to the mighty power
of time; it also experiments with an art of speed, it tries out an
art of *lifting* [vol] (in the sense of the *furtive* robber adept at steal-
ing very quickly, in an instant, before time could find the time
to turn back, but also in the sense of the flight [*vol*] and the flapping wing). An art of flying and thieving this fleeting touch *of*
eternity is, yes, an art of the aerial movement, of what holds itself
aloft with a single breath or a single flap of the wing, at the moment when the angelic, secret wing of eternity comes to caress
you, for this is also an art of caressing, and eternity touches us,
in this "fleeting touch *of* eternity," barely touches you, without us
touching on eternity, according to a caress that you know, not so
much how to hold back, that would be vulgar, but how to feel.
Remember the "touch with flapping wings" of Rilke's angel (*mit
fernen, mit Flügelschlägen*). Now this "fleeting touch of eternity"
at the speed of time, I would like to see it transmute in a flash,
without too much artifice, into "bonds of immortality" a few lines
further down. "We manufacture bonds of immortality," she says.
In the meantime, and that would justify my aero- or ethero-dy-
namic reading of the "fleeting touch of eternity," figures she calls
stuntmen, who hold on to one another by the thread of a letter,
are seen flying through the air.

> They come and go on the void provided they are weighted with a
> letter. A piece of paper. Preferably recent. Everything in history hangs
> on speech. Doctors would say so: sometimes one dies for a word, for
> a word one does not die, one waits, sometimes in the middle of a
> sentence, always for a sentence, one is lost, saved.

This is, at least in this passage, one of the first salutations to the word "saved [*sauvé*]." Now it will rebound, yes, the letter of this word is awaiting us, it will rebound to the letter on the facing page ("At the sight of the envelope, one is saved already"). With this doctor's quotation ("Doctors would say so: sometimes one dies for a word . . . "), you know, if you have read *OR*, that a reference is made to the paradigm of Georges and of the death of the father. A paradigm that would be enough, if one so wished, to reveal the original crossing of this book, *OR*, with the great modern filiation, that of the phthisical or consumptive space of literature, adding this singular masterpiece to the flowers of consumptive evil. Tuberculosis and asthma: Kafka, Mann, Proust, Blanchot. But just time enough to bring to mind a whole stream of questions: What is a *reference* (I have just said: "A reference is made to the paradigm of Georges and of the death of the father")? But also, what is a paradigm? And who is Georges? And the father, and the death of the father? Especially if "no dead person has ever said their last word,"[113] whereas such and such a man held to be alive may have said a last word that nobody has heard. What is a last word, then, or a next to last word? The critics and theorists of literature who, in academia or in periodicals of all kinds, would like to know the meaning and the reference, the what and the who of this book— and of so many others—had better learn to relearn everything.

Here are now, following after the "fleeting touch of eternity," the "bonds of immortality":

> After a while, like all words the thread gets worn [the thread of the stuntmen, I suppose, and the wire of the funambulists, and it is always the finitude of time—JD]. It is the human paradox: we manufacture bonds of immortality. They work. During an indeterminate length of time, immortality is guaranteed. [Finite, provisional immortality.—JD] But one must reckon with the innumerable forces of Death. The latter does not remain inactive. It persecutes politically morally professionally it comes near the body dangerously.[114]

This last sentence, alone, which acknowledges the persecuting work of Death, with *D* capitalized, a breath-taking persecution I will speak about again, is written in one stroke, without punctuation, without allowing time to breathe: "It persecutes politically morally professionally it comes near the body dangerously."

On the following page, without delaying, what does she write, as if to describe these "bonds of immortality"?

"Bonds of immortality," written *b-o-n-d-s*; if I dared, I would change their spelling to "bounds," *b-o-u-n-d-s*, in order to make this *bon mot* also sound, *volens nolens*, like the incredible bound that a standing jump into immortality can take away [*enlever*] from time, thus itself soaring [*s'enlevant*] mightily from the ground of time, where it takes off, at one go, soaring, rising [*s'élevant*], taking flight [*s'envolant*], lifting itself away [*se volant*] in a single bound, taking time, taking time from time, lifting [*volant*] it from time, outspeeding time, for that takes time, taking all the time it needs, because time is lacking, the time to take time by surprise, at one go [*d'un coup*], at a single glance [*d'un seul coup d'oeil*] (*Augenblick*) or with a single flap of the wing [*d'un seul coup d'aile*], "fleeting touch of eternity": we will be immortal in a moment but only the time of the bound, and even also, to speak one of her many tongues, English, the immortal time of a *bond, b-o-n-d,* of a tie, a promise, a commitment, of an "*engagement" for life,* that is to say, the whole of life but also in favor of life, of an act of faith in fiding [*fiance*], "would that might might [*la puisse la puissance*]," the time from which one takes off to leap with such a bound becoming nothing but a token of eternity, nothing more, nothing less, a trick played on persecution, the very defeat of persecution.

One could call that the *bondir* [bounding] of Hélène Cixous, but this time writing the verb with an *e* at the end; then *bondire* would substitute itself for benedicence [*bien dire*] or for speaking good [*dire du bien*] in order to signal, with a bound, toward benediction. With a feline bound, like a cat or like a tiger. The *bondire* of Hélène Cixous would have the mighty powers or the virtues of a benediction. How so?

On the opposite page, facing us, therefore, here is first, in order to put the "*bonds of immortality*" back into circulation, to narrate and literalize this *bondire* of blessed immortality, the anticipated *je vis*, a "*Je vis des lettres* [I live on / saw letters]," which, as a general motto of Hélène Cixous's would do, designates twice at once: the motto designates, at this precise moment, the letters that arrive or do not arrive at their destination through the infinitely fast pace of a mail; but the motto also designates, leaping as ever with a flap of the wing above epistolary order, literally the literality of all the letters of the alphabet: writing itself.

Now here, and again I must interrupt the bounding leap, I must immobilize the image—and the hand still trembles as it carves out shadows and figures, and underlines *must* [il faut] three times:

> I live on / saw letters. One cannot ask for them. As they are graces, they **must** arrive. For them to be graces, they **must** arrive **when they must**: at the last minute. I myself cannot predict the last minute. For it always comes upon us without warning. But your letter arrives just before.

These three times "must [*il faut*]" are brought to bear on things and times each time different. They do tell of [*disent bien*] the might and infinite acceleration of the "might": would that the letters might arrive. In arriving, the letters are the events, the very figures of the event, like the *arrivant*: like the letter, the event is a thing "*made to* arrive." The omnipotence of the "might" is brought to bear above all else on the arriving [*arrivance*] of the letter as well as of the event. And now, hey presto, you're going to see that the "might" really works. The letter arrives *since it must* arrive, and when it must.

But then what are the graces thus granted ("For them to be graces, they must arrive when they must: at the last minute")? An event, like a benediction, can only be a grace, namely that which happens or arrives just where not expected, when one no longer anticipates or calculates anything: failing which nothing happens/ arrives to the letter. The graces thus granted have the grace of a meaning that disseminates itself at the multiple crossings of its genealogy. Graces give or receive and therefore happen/arrive more than once: the grace of what is given, first, graciously, gratuitously, without exchange, arriving as pure donation where, like everything that arrives, one does not expect it; then the grace of the dance, in accordance with the choreographic writing I was just speaking about; then especially, shall I say, as the end, in the end, the grace that pardons [*gracie*] at the last minute. The first two graces gave and danced without pardoning, that is to say, without doing what grace does when one spares or pardons by an act of grace [*quand on fait grâce ou quand on gracie*]—for example, a man sentenced to death. Now here grace gives in all senses, it gives birth but it also pardons by a sovereign act of grace, it grants life by interrupting dying [*mourance*], it lifts the sentence and literally gives life *again*, forgives, gives itself without reserve body and soul (what *perdonare* should say), and, at the last minute, it gives and forgives life as for the first time, life *for* life. In order to begin approaching what, it seems to me, remains to be thought of what I call "life *for* life" here, one must surrender, yes, surrender, and all the genius of the address lies in *rendering oneself* and *surrendering* [se rendre], an-other untranslatable verb: in French *se rendre* is to give oneself up to, to abandon oneself to, to give oneself over, to give oneself, un-conditionally, but also to know where to betake oneself, to know where one goes, and to go there, to know how to gain the address: to surrender is to gain—a terrifying truth. As I was saying, in or-der to begin approaching truth—what, it seems to me, remains to be thought, which I call "life *for* life" here—one must surrender or render oneself to the alliance of these two graces, in two senses, according to two gracious virtues of grace, that of the gift or of choreography (the noun without a verb) and that which, in con-cord with [*accordée à*] the act of the transitive verb, pardons some-one, grants [*accorde*] life and saves the other at the last moment. And for life. Besides, we already had to suspend this distinction between the noun and the verb: the nominalization of the verb, the appellation of the proper noun, nomination as appellation, is the noun made verb or the verb made noun; it is the action of the *making live* or of the *giving of life*, even of resurrecting through the appellation of the proper noun—and that is grace that pardons. You could have read an example of it on the next to last page of

OR—from which I quote a few lines without any commentary at all, even where I am sure that centuries of meticulous reading could well find employment. I carve out the fragment in such a way as to be able to extract and underline in the middle of it, not far from "this grace," the phrase "joy of vital assent," which matters to me for reasons that are I hope starting to become clear. Here are, then, on a certain date, at a certain address, the two graces in one, at the last minute, on the next to last page:

> I am now thrown backward in the opposite direction. In the next blast I catch an envelope . . .

There had already been blasts; they had blown [*souffler*] previously in the same paragraph, which itself came after a paragraph naming the "vital breath [*souffle*] of the book." A blast, therefore, an irreplaceably powerful word, which also tells of the overthrowing power of a rainy wind; this word travels at the speed of the wind, in a flurry [*en coup de vent*]. Remember, a few pages earlier, it was already the wind: "My life depends on my address [*je vis d'adresse*]" was followed, precisely to explain and describe the address, by an allusion to this skillful movement of address, which consists in going like the wind and faster than the wind, in gaining speed over the wind and doing so in one word ("to toss the word over the wind," she says), as if the word, in one word, gained in speed on the wind, gained on the wind at the speed of light which makes visible without delay. So she said, a few pages earlier: "My life depends on my address. To toss the word over the wind and to receive the letter absolutely without fail long before it appears before my face." What appears before my face, faster than the wind, therefore arrives before arriving, at the moment when the word has just left: it arrives while leaving. The letter comes in front of me before the wind. Before the wind, it comes upon me. I resume my quotation about the last-minute blast, on the next to last page:

> I am now thrown backward in the opposite direction. In the next blast I catch ["catch" once again: she catches all the time—JD] an envelope. I open it—the date is April 11, 1935. The first sentence takes

me. It is a force. It carries me away in three words beyond any apprehension. I was not expecting such a grace . . .

A grace that is given to her, no doubt, the gift and the unexpected salvation that at the last minute saves the man sentenced to death in a sovereign manner. But first and foremost, grace also as the very beauty of the letter or of the first sentence of the letter. Grace is not only what it receives as a last-minute gracious gift, the gift of life, but the character, the property, the form, the essence of what it is given and what is in itself, like a letter, like this sentence, a grace. Which she is indeed going to analyze and describe straightaway. I resume and continue my quotation:

> I was not expecting such a grace. Such proportions. A fearful symmetry. The bearing of this apparition. It is a thing of beauty. The nobility of this syntax, the uprightness of this adjusted step. Its rhythm is familiar to me it is that of the ancient affirmation of being. What a neat inflexible thing led in the brightness of an obedience to the Idea of Good. One can sense the rigor of the subject of enunciation, a taste for the meter. This is a model.
>
> Beyond what it says, the sentence takes off and draws the Beginning the Body and the End in pure space. At the sight of this figure, I feel the joy of vital assent. How beautiful you are, I cried out . . . [115]

Vital assent: how beautiful you are, sentence, figure, life, life for life, lively [*vivement*]. O that there be life [*vivement la vie*]. Not life for life against death, life in exchange for death, life *for* death (we are also following the paradigm of the father sentenced to death, a paradigm according to which everything substitutes itself in accordance with the great genius of substitution), but life *for* life. Besides, the grace that, by the grace of the letter, pardons the father, albeit after his death, still obeys two kinds of logic. This is very well explained in a passage from *OR* that, once again, literally alternates between "on the one hand [*d'un côté*] . . . " and "but on the other hand [*mais d'un autre côté*] . . . ":

> On the one hand [these are her words—JD] . . . , in the hallucinatory projection . . . , my father would be in my desire. . . . But on

the other hand, there was already, in the past, in the very structure of what he lived in the present, the possibility of this other presence.[116]

In other words, what I do with my father, for my father's life, well, my father, maybe, the mighty power of my father's presence will already have done it beforehand for life, for my life. And what I would have liked to talk to you about is this musical inflection of the enchanting chant that changes everything, this downpour of the *pour* [for], which tips the *pour* from one meaning to the other when grace dances, gives and forgives for life. For life and unto death.

Thus act the "mighty lives," as is said in *OR*. In *Savoir*, written more or less at the same time, she designates "the mightiest hands." Thus act the mightiest hands. And thus act, in *OR*, at the speed at which she lives them, the "letters of omnipotence."

> The letters of omnipotence are small in size naturally. High-speed notes. At the sight of the envelope, one is already saved. Then comes joy. It will say:

A colon and a blank, new paragraph (one must always respect the space and the suspension of this typographical notation):

> It will say: "I don't want to die." It is your letter: "Do so that I don't die." I do. I give Death the order not to take a step. It is enough to ask and not to want. Blessed be the bridegroom who does not want, but the one who asks will be saved . . .

"Blessed be the bridegroom . . . ," my spelling was not so wrong or artificial when, a moment ago, it skipped, from bond to bound, then to *bondir* [bounding] without an *e*, then with a leap, from *bondir* to *bon-dire* [benedicence], and from *bondire* to benediction. From one page to the next, the transmutation had worked on its own in silence, from the bond of immortality into a benediction. Thus she writes:

> Blessed be the bridegroom who does not want, but the one who asks will be saved. The letter says: "Hold me above the jaws" and I do so. "Replace the time gone by" and I replace it. I have the power: you

just have to ask for it. The power of love is older than the moon and than death and younger than time.

I have not begun yet, forgive me. But "for life," in the title I proposed, signals perhaps, at a stroke, unwittingly and unintentionally, toward the *bondire* and the benediction of what is said *of* this letter and first *to* this letter of survival. Of this letter and to this letter.

For she always speaks to the letter.

But I am not sure of my reading. Who could be? Who could assume the right to inscribe the archive of this letter? And first, to do that, to identify it in the infinite play of substitution of letters that Hélène Cixous's opus operates, she who knows how to replace everything, at full speed, including time and death, by the bond of an immortality? Substitution is her top game, the power and magic of this writing, of what happens or takes place, miraculously, through the mighty power of substitution, but of a substitution that leaves the living itself [*vivant singulier*] in place. Thus the latter is kept alive or given back to life through the grace of a bound. At an infinite speed, on the instant, in a single bound. Never forget the subtitle of her great book on Joyce, which was her first book and, according to me, the first book worthy of this name and worthy of Joyce in France: *L'Exil de Joyce ou l'art du remplacement,* Joyce's exile being itself replaced, on the spot, by the gesture of a simple "*ou* [or]," by the art of substitution: the exile of James Joyce *or* the art of substitution.[117]

Now, then, she replaces everything, from one hour to the next: "Replace the time gone by," says the letter. The voice replies: "And I replace. I have the power."

But this power to replace, *just by taking place,* is not incompatible; on the contrary, it goes hand in hand with the acute experience of election, of the unique and the irreplaceable, of the innumerable as irreplaceable. Similarly, this "I have the power" ("And I replace. I have the power") goes hand in hand with the confession of an equally indisputable unpower—which, I suppose, she would be the last to want to dispute. Indeed, and I am getting there, she occasionally writes "without my being able to do anything about it." My thesis is that this "without my being able to do anything about it" in no way contradicts the mighty power of the "might."

What is this unpower, then, this limit to the mighty power of whatever writing might do? This "I have the power" is completed here by the possessive or the verbal phrase, by a strange verb, by the verbal noun of a strange operation that any power perhaps amounts to, namely substitution, the "power to replace." Now this "I have the power" goes hand in hand with the destiny of "without my being able to do anything about it." For the power I have, the power to replace, is not mine. It has been given to me like a grace and I myself am the unique substitute of a letter, of an order, of an injunction, of a responsibility, of a heritage that I am/follow to the letter.

In this substitution of letters that yet remain in their place, I do not know where to place the one, always unique letter, this letter that is thus countersigned by the benediction. I am not sure she knows it or wants to know it herself. Is it a single missing letter or not? Or else a single absolute letter? Or else the single letter that I myself am? These three hypotheses come one after another in sequence like the same and the other in accordance with the metonymic braid that unfolds over three pages from *OR*.[118]

1. First, the missing letter—well before any purloined letter:

> WE WERE MISSING A LETTER. There was a letter. It was the last and only one, it was missing from the triumph of our game. . . . We summoned the omission to disgorge [*rendre gorge*].

Rendre gorge is but one of the six hundred instances of *gorge* [throat]. *Gorge* almost sounds like a first name.

2. The absolute letter. Why did Georges not leave us an absolute letter?

> If we had been my father, I would have left an absolute letter before leaving. One letter for all the darkness. I could see it very well. One letter for all the chapters. The last sentence. I could see it very well. I could imagine this letter. . . . It would say:

And after a blank, a quasi-citation of the fictional letter of which I had already read a part and which says:

> Mighty are the places it haunts. . . . Mighty the spirit of the letter.

3. Finally the letter that I am/follow:

> I am/follow myself your letter to me I said.[119]

An infinite sentence in its unstable syntax: a narcissistic closure or exactly the opposite, which amounts to the same as much as to the other: your letter comes to me at once, without delay, because it is already me, in me, etc.. Tautology and autonomy. One does not know whether it is the father who addresses her—in her—or whether she addresses her father in her. She knows without knowing. But conversely, I am/follow myself your letter to me, for I am only the letter you send me, I am only *insofar as and where* I receive a letter from you, I am nothing without it, nothing in this vulnerable exposure of myself to a letter from you, on the absolutely other side. I am not, I have no relationship to myself before receiving a letter from you in me. Dissymetry, this time, heterology and absolute heteronymy. There is only one side, mine, but it is on your side, on the side of your side, on the spot, in a moment, all for your moment [*sur l'heure, tout à l'heure, toute à ton heure*].

Hence omnipotence as impotence, the experience of the impossible. The letter from you, which I am/follow, I cannot touch it, I cannot do anything about it, it is without my being able to do anything about it. If the mighty power of the "might" arises and appears, it is precisely where I can do nothing, where the indicative power of the "I can" risks the experience and *experils* its limit. She says:

> It never occurred to me while reading that I could change a line a sentence a breath of the book, that is to say of a written being. Even when a book attacks me or offends me. The book is without my **being able to do** anything about it. There is no animate thing more

absolute finite external to me. . . . The animate written thing is stone
and God. I bow in front of it.[120]

The mighty power of the *might* lifts itself [*se vole*], it flies away
[*s'envole*] where that happens/arrives, or does not, without my being able to do anything about it. With my *not* being able to do
anything about it. I will leave the expletive negation its mighty
power of indecision.[121] Here is *Anankè*. And I begin reading, what
is called reading, what *is* (written) only when all the mighty power
of the "might," far from being annihilated by the limit it comes
up against in what is (written), which I can do nothing about because it has already happened, is then measured against the impossible and enjoys it, jubilantly, and answers "yes." Difficult to
say whether it is life or death, whether it is avoided, denied, or
acknowledged, or acknowledged through the strange event or the
strange element of this denial that is not a renegation. The act
of faith, believing only can decide, without norms and without a
program, by a commitment of life to life and unto death, whether
it will be life or death.

Might [puisse] forms and constitutes an event in itself; it is even
the performative par excellence, the performativity of a performative that precedes and conditions any other performative and
therefore any event; there is no performative that does not imply a
"would that might happen/arrive," "would it, he, she, might hap-
pen/arrive." But there are events that are not connected to per-
formatives, and these are even the most event-like events, those
that happen or arrive to us, and the *arrivants* who happen/arrive
to us where we do not perform anything any longer, despite any
possible performative: such is the place of the necessary impossible, of *anankè* or of *tukhè*, of fate, of impotence, which is not the
opposite of the possible and of potency. Neither a promise nor a
messianic expectation, the un-formed, not even my monstrosity:
life death, the exhaustion of the sun before its time or a definitive
prosthesis of the sun.

Now, watch out, since we are dealing with denial and renegation, allow me to play the prophet a little longer for my next to last

beginning. A moment ago, with regard to the eco-homonymy of speed, the impossible translation and all the resistances to brotherly transferences [*transfrères*], all the events that such untranslatability never fails to program, I announced that I will say a few words about the place of this-life-these-works in History, with a capital *H*.

Only a few words, too brief, a programmatic as much as a prophetic note.

I foresee, therefore, and I foretell, I announce what will take place one day, when one reads her [*quand on la lira*] at last. "One will read her," this impersonal future does not mean that she will have been read by nobody so far. Far from that, and we are testifying to that at present. The private, even secret and singular reading remains *de rigueur*, and it is an adventure about which I have nothing to say, within myself, for others than myself. Rather "one will read her" designates the moment when a certain public, shared reading of her work will have crossed a threshold of recognition—this most strange word (*Anerkennung*), which we have just touched on in the uncle's language. Then this singular work will not only be read by a happy few, by which I mean not an elite but the first allies of this power, those who will have had what we called above the "courage" to accord themselves this mighty power and to accord themselves with it; and that presupposes a great many conditions, so many chances or graces that I will not enumerate. This courage or this grace can be given unpredictably to readers, male or female, which nothing seems to prepare for that: their situation, competence, social or linguistic position from one end of the world to the other, institutional knowledge or national culture.

I foresee and I foretell, I announce that, then, once this threshold has been crossed, one will not only decipher in this very work the law and the meaning of all the historical resistances that will have opposed its recognition, even its legitimation. The work will also serve as an analyzer and, one might say, as a seer or signal—for the work watches like a seer or a signal—for whoever would seek to identify those resistances and to account for them. In a quasi-scientific way.

Oh, we know that well, some will indeed say, the work of Hélène Cixous and she as a person do not have to wait for this future-to-come, they already have an incontestable legitimacy: French, European, and worldwide fame. She is already very highly rated (I am speaking here of the rating or *cote*, which is neither *la côte du côté* [the rib of the side] nor the coat of mail [*cotte de mailles*] but, to use another spelling, the quoting of the share [*la cotation de la* quote-part], of the *quota*, the measure of a valuation, of quoting, of a *quotation*—it is the same word—the quantitative distribution of stocks and shares on the market of fame). To which I will reply: it is true, her fame is great, but let us not be deceived by this world rating, by this share of authority in the world of literature, of theater, of politics, of so-called feminist theory, in the academic world, the old world and the new world, and the third world (which already add up to more than the "two worlds" of her childhood in Oran). The rating of this worldwide recognition, as we witness it, must not conceal what remains in our eyes a fierce ignorance and an irredentist resistance to reading. Would it might be analyzed one day. The day when this interminable analysis begins, but it is not just around the corner, I presume it will have to answer thousands of questions or six hundred charges, no doubt (which I must leave to their reserve here). Above all, it will need not to fail, not to fall, if that is possible, into some traps or *tests*, which are all the more perverse since the devices of these traps are set within one another. I can only identify the outlines of these three or four traps or tests, which will put her to the test, in one word.

1. I put in the first place the event of poetic power, by which I mean the business of writing, and language. Why in the first place, and also, therefore, last? Certainly, the resistances-ignorances that we are speaking of are numerous and overdetermined. No doubt they stand, as they accumulate, at the crossroads of several armed forces. First there is the armed force of misogyny or of phallogocentrism—to give it a name too hastily—which cannot acknowledge might on the other side of sexual difference and sometimes

pretends to escape this old program only to worsen and capitalize its profits, an operation that can find strategists among *both* men *and* women. There is also the strategic force of media, journalism, and publishing, whose machinery is in fact programmed by this same program. Then one must reckon with what welds these two machinations to the academic machinery and to all national cultures, starting of course with French culture, since it is the sensitive spot, which, because it is the closest—according to a law we know well, a familiar and family law that applies also to all close relatives [*les proches*], and first of all to the family—precisely remains the site of the most resisting resistance. The avoidance is first of all in the family, even if it also propagates, little by little [*de proche en proche*], in the geopolitical field. All that would be rather easy to show and illustrate with innumerable examples and signs. It would be enough to read the newspapers, the majority of newspapers and even of specialized newspapers, with the ratings [*cotes*] they publish every day. Allow me not to speak about it. All of this is too obvious. What is less easy to show is the last resort, the common resource of all these refusals to legitimize the work of a woman who is not only and at once, simultaneously, a great professor who has stirred things up in a thousand ways on the academic front, innovating in France and in Europe, not only in Vincennes-Saint-Denis, in women's studies, or at the Collège International de Philosophie, *and* a great critic, *and* a great man of the theater who has renewed the whole notion of the theater, *and* a great poet or a great unclassifiable writer, *and* a man of action, the dedicated militant for a great number of causes—which, thank God, we often had in common (May 1968, the GIP,[122] apartheid and Mandela, and not only the cause of women or of other, often undocumented [*sans papiers*][123] victims of persecution throughout the world, so often but not only in Algeria, and the International Parliament of Writers[124]—the list would be too long here). This would already be too much for a single man, this is intolerable for a woman. Now what do the ultimate resource, the arsenal or the absolute weapon of these armed forces, the common source of these strategies of avoidance or denials come down to or amount to? Well, always to what is the opposite of a mighty power, to an impotence faced with writing, to the im-potency of reading, that is to say also to the lack of what is called, in this new meaning of the word we glimpsed a moment ago, *courage*, the heart [*coeur*], the *courage* to surrender or render oneself, through repression, to what takes place here in language, to the enchanting chant of what happens to and through language, to the words, the nouns, the verbs, and finally to the element of the letter, of the homonym "letter" as it is put to work here, to what signs an experience of coming to grips with the untranslatability of the idiom, which, through the chain of replacements, homophonymies, metonymic substitutions, gear changes, infringements of all the major codes, knows how to produce unique events, insofar as they call the best protected securities into question once and for all: genre, *gender*, filiation, proper noun, identity, cultural heritage, the distinction between faith and knowledge, between theory and practice, between philosophy, psychoanalysis, and literature, between historical memory and political urgency, etc.; so many boundaries whose crossing one can follow only if one is an expert, at one's own risk, in each of these territories and in crossing their limits in an experilous way, etc.. All this is rarely given, it is at once a grace and tremendous work (she does a tremendous amount of work in all these domains: to take this one example, she reads more history to prepare a given play than an army of historians, and that applies to all domains, without talking about other aspects of her work). Now within this first test (what I call the first test of the first trap), not only are all the other tests, which I will define in a moment, accumulated in potentiality [*en puissance*], in reserve, but insofar as they all work through untranslatable writing, through the enchanting chant of the letter in the elemental seismic meaning I have just spoken about, the test of translation has its place not only between the French language (the dominant language of her work) and other languages. The test takes place inside (if there is one) the aforesaid French language, and it is yet more treacherous and more unrecognizable, more decisive, for it first touches the body of her writing. It is as if, since they do not read her, the

French quoted or quoting [*cotés ou cotant*] on the stock exchange were for the moment reproaching Hélène Cixous with being untranslatable into French. Which is true in another way. The discourses of quotation [*cotation*] cannot translate her, and therefore first read her in the code of their quote [*cote*]. I could provide a thousand illustrations of this, but I will not for lack of time. In short, one day this work will be the analyzer of the conditions of its own ignorance. One will ask oneself: what must have been the culture—the media, publishing, academic culture; in a word, culture—of this country whose language she is said to speak whereas one has not been able, nor known how, nor wanted, to hear, see, and read her in it? What is it that this national culture made a point of refusing? Not of refusing to celebrate or even to fear, with all sorts of ambiguous bowing and scraping, but of refusing to lay itself open to the mighty power of the enchanting chant, of refusing what I call here the countersigning reading?

I will insist rather on the other side of the same test. Certainly, those men and women who organize a declared resistance do not read her. But conversely, those men and women who do not read her, even if they declare themselves to be her allies or friends in all fields (of politics, academe, publishing, the theater), are not merely her allies: they also belong, whether they like and know it or not, to the camp of the resistance, by lending a hand or a foot to it. From there I move on to the second test.

2. That is to say, inside, to what happens on the other side. As I am speaking now about resistance from the inside, in the camp of the friends and allies, it goes without saying that I neither exclude nor exculpate myself. I am not denouncing a resistance from the outside, condemning it or attacking it as one would an evil, like an evil of which anyone would be innocent. This resistance is also a fatality. My own reading, as the years went by, has been nothing but a long experience of more or less successfully overcome resistances, and it will be so for life. She herself is not innocent of it, and, from one place or one degree of power to the other, she resists herself by herself. She has explained this division very

well. She must resist herself, if I may say so, avoid herself, forget
herself or forgetread herself [*s'oublire*], fail to know herself in order
to continue. Each of her works is a body, some of whose more or
less powerful sites resist others, which are more or less powerful,
and the work, or what I call by this uncertain word, the work at
work represents a relatively stabilized balance, from one book to
the next, from one unit to the next, in the midst of this conflict
between resistances that resist themselves, by themselves against
themselves. Resistance always resists more or less well, first of all
against itself, more or less powerfully. And more is less here. A
resistance is never simple, and might is always a play of resistances
with an intensity differential. Resistance begins by resisting itself,
and that is why denegation and denial are lodged at the heart of
acknowledgment (the *no* of *Verleugnen* must continue to torment
the *yes* of *Anerkennen* from within, just as de-negation [*le dé-renier*]
must continue to torment renegation [*le renier*], etc.).

Having said that, this single, double, triple precaution having
been taken, let us not overindulge in it and so neglect far more
massive forms of the aforesaid internal resistance, whose main
places (once one has taken into account all the others I have just
spoken about under the heading of transferential phallogocentrism)
are first of all, in this internal war, the dominant places of, say,
the feminist institution in all its forms, wherever, in the name of
woman, a regime [*pouvoir*] sets up its machinery for appropriation,
inspection, and capitalization. The most blatant figure is the army,
the armed woman who, without reading, without translating the
enchanting chant of letter and language, finds her paltry stratagem
and her allies in the reductive manipulation that consists in clas-
sifying the name and the work of Hélène Cixous among the "great-
French-women-theorists-of-the-feminine" (feminine-writing,
feminine-sexuality, etc.). You know only too well the taxonomic
column of this blacklisting under cover of a laudatory reference:
the list of French theorists I, J, K, X, Y, Z or X, Y, Z, A, B, C. It
is not solely American, but it is first of all massively so; and if it is
not an academic battlefield, it is at least a quotation [*cotation*] or a
coterie on campus. As always when coming from the United States,

the investment becomes global and in the process of [*en cours de*] globalization, at the rate and quoted price [*au cours et à la cote*] of globalization in progress [*en cours*]. Then, without reading her and being able to translate her, one pigeonholes her in the family of the great-militant-French-feminist-theorists-of-the-thing-called-woman—which she is too but not only. Thus one can see her name appear in a series of authors' names that have little in common with her, the last thing they share with her being precisely the work of writing. Mireille Calle-Gruber said it very well, among so many other things, in her fine book. (This sometimes happens to names of French men cited abroad in an immutable series. I, for my part, know that this somnambulistic moment means that reading has not begun or has already stopped—and, in fact, it gives me the clearest signal that it must stop. For me, reading stops as soon as I see these columns of names on the march: I turn the page over or close the book, I zap.) But again, if this is macroscopic, massive, and too visible in the United States, from the United States, the same resistance is at work on the side of the French allies through finer filters, subtly, suggestively, silently. Silently both because one does not hear it and because first of all this resistance does not hear. It works toward silencing the enchanting chant. One sometimes celebrates and recognizes *with a view* to not hearing, not letting one hear, or not giving one to hear, to the point of silencing. Once again, I do not denounce the aforesaid resistance and I claim a part in this responsibility. Besides, in calling upon the analysis (to come) of these silencing resistances, I wish above all to remain positive and, beyond all ambivalences, salute the friends, both men and women, of Hélène Cixous. One must, without resentment, pay homage and express one's gratitude to all those men and women who, particularly in France, have had the courage, if only in resisting with the courage of a resistance fighter, to ally themselves with Hélène Cixous, to pledge themselves, to commit themselves, while taking serious risks, to somebody and to a work by which, at the same time, the time of this risk, these persons and institutions were truly inspired to be inspired. The debt incurred through these very resistances, and therefore the price to pay, remains incalculable on

both sides, as is the chance given on either side. I have in mind Antoinette Fouque and the whole adventure of Des Femmes (which I
find hard to imagine without Hélène Cixous); Ariane Mnouchkine
and the Théâtre du Soleil (which I find hard to imagine without
Hélène Cixous); Daniel Mesguich and more than one theater—in
short, all these places where, each time, according to me, events
have disrupted the very space where they were occurring by leaving
shock waves whose scale one has not assessed yet.[125] In particular, I would have liked to speak about the plays of these last years,
namely *La Ville parjure* and *L'Histoire (qu'on ne connaîtra jamais)*,
which for me were among the most disturbing experiences of theater and thoughtful thought ever. Here I have neither the time nor
the desire to go into details about these "allied" resistances and the
kind of avoidance that is allied to recognition, in academia, in the
theater, in publishing, etc.. This takes us back to what is closer to
us, around here, in this very room, and first of all to the place from
which I myself am speaking and have to calculate even my very
prophecies. But this gives me a transition to define the third test—
trapped or trapping.

3. As we learn from her uncle, who knew a good bit about it,
acknowledgment itself is a powerful act of avoidance. It unties
[*dénoue*] and analyzes only by denying and renegating [*dénier et
renier*] (*anerkennen, beugen, widersetzen*: at once to acknowledge,
bend, bow in front of—death or greatness, *Anankè*—and at the
same time, not to do it, to oppose it, mis-recognize, resist, avoid,
renege de-negation [*dé-reniement*]). This is inscribed right into the
might of might, where the *yes* of enjoying might [*puissance jouis-
sique*] and of jussory enjoyment [*jouissance jussique*] exposes itself
experilously to difference *in* might and even to the eschatology of
the impossible. It cannot be otherwise. that is what *Anankè*, the
common noun, the proper noun and what is named by the title of
a book, also means.

4. Fourth test of the trap, metalanguage or what one should
rather call here metaphrase. *Metaphrasis* is the Greek word for

translation, what passes from one language or one phrase to the other by the transference of a "that is to say." *Metaphrasô*: I transport from one phrase or one language into another, I paraphrase, I periphrase, I translate, I work through the metaphrastic copula of a "that is," through the operator of a "that is to say." Resistances, the denials in acknowledgment we are speaking of here, are to be found at the crossroads of metalanguage and metaphrastic translation, at the passage of the "that is to say." To have a chance of overcoming such an invincible resistance (since it resists itself by itself, and therefore one never stops beginning again with it), it is not enough to read. Nor even to write *on the subject of* what one reads. In order to read, one must write, sign something else, and the impossible belief I was speaking about presupposes the pledge of this other language, which must at once be other in countersigning what it listens to and metaphrases as it speaks. And therefore one must do something, make let something happen/arrive [*faire laisser arriver*] while speaking about something, even while speaking another language on the subject of another language. This confirms once more that there is no place for a metalanguage here but that one cannot abandon this certainty to its own facility. There is also a necessity for metalanguage, that is to say, for a language that speaks of a language, its own or another, if only to hear/understand its meaning and give one to hear/understand its law, even formalize it. Simply, as an effect, this metaphrastic moment is comprehended in the differential of the mighty powers of *might*. A metalanguage or a metaphrase always tends to overbid and exceed in might [*en puissance*] the "might" from which it draws [*puise*] and above whose well [*puits*] it claims to rise in order to speak its truth. To get the truth out of the well. The truth of the essence, what one says when one says *it/that is* [c'est], is only an agency in the differential of the intensities of power. The "that is" of the "that is to say" is often the most powerful. "It is so, as one says, that's what it is, I'm telling you; that's indeed what it does or what it means, even if it is a prodigy or a miracle, let us note and let us be aware." But mightier than what the "that is" speaks about, the "that is," "that is to say" still remains a mighty power, a phenomenon of power. This puts us back on the track of a mighty power that must be thought before and at the heart of any so-called will to power or possibility of the "might." And this very *thought* of might remains a mighty power—in potentiality as well as in actuality.

What can I possibly do, given how far I am in my prophecy? I know, up to a point, what I am doing or what I have just attempted. While claiming to announce, predict, or prophesy the future-to-come of H.C., I cannot but lend a hand to it and cannot avoid the fact that already, in the guise I lend to it, it begins around here. I take part, at least, in the provocation of what I pretend to predict. But *on the one hand*, I should not confess this concession, if that belongs to all those truths about which I said to myself one must not declare them at the border and which I could yet not help displaying; *on the other hand*, I am anything but sure of the future-to-come thus announced. I simply say: I believe in it and would it might happen. Oh, I wish it might happen.

Yes, I am telling you it will happen.

Anyway, nobody is obliged to believe me.

But do put yourself to the test, if you can and have the courage, watch out, you'll see what you'll see and you'll read what you'll read.

I'll begin again.

Here is at last my last beginning. It takes the narration of my story back to the time and place that I had planned to take as my starting point, namely the first book, *Le Prénom de Dieu* (1967), which I had first thought of falling back on while beating a retreat in front of the intimidating vastness of her work. I had said to myself: I will only speak of this first book, that will make a nice beginning, I will leave the rest intact and virgin for a reading entirely to come—and I will also speak of the beginnings of what was also for me only the beginning, soon after the appointment at the Balzar.

For my first concern will have been for anamnesis and to begin understanding at last what may have happened for her since that time. And for me. And my desire was to remember, through a memory at once active and patchy, deceitful, reconstructed, maybe hallucinated and filled with wonder, what my first reading of her first book will have truly been, for example, without retrospective illusion. To tell you the truth in a nutshell, in two words, on the one hand I can remember only a spectral outline of it, and I am going to describe it to you. On the other hand, and this is what matters to me more, I have the impression that I start being able and knowing how to read this first book only today, some thirty-five years later. And what I have said so far was merely a preparatory move, for me in any case; with a view to the time when, in a moment, I start beginning again to read *Le Prénom de Dieu* in this very place.

Some time after the appointment at the Balzar, for we had to see each other again, the author left a manuscript in my care. The author had not published anything yet, nor signed H.C., and, short of doing things her own way, would have nearly signed H.B., as did a certain Stendhal about whom the author decided to speak here in 1992, under the pretext of myself—and of a crest. The author had not even published *L'Exil de James Joyce ou l'art du remplacement* yet, which may have been, in a certain way, a kind of workshop, cellar, forge, or forgery where all the resources have not been produced, certainly (and in a way she owes nothing to Joyce, whom she does not like much), but where a kind of historical test or dress rehearsal was settling scores with so many programs from past literature. This book on Joyce was like the passage through the exhaustion of a historical culture, an immense act of memory of all the memories, the fiction of a first night or of a dress rehearsal on the following day of which one was going at last to play not *this* play—oh, what a surprise for the spectators and the critics!—but another, an entirely other play. Point taken. Only on this account, and to start from it, this great book on Joyce remains in 1998 an indispensable experimental laboratory for whoever wants to understand what followed, and not forget that her part 1, the matrix or patrix of all the *sides* to come, is entitled "John Joyce:

The Father's Side [*Du côté de John Joyce: Le parti pris du père*]," a chapter in which you would learn that "James [Joyce] never repudiated his father in real life, and hardly even in his works," and the same part 1, "The Family Cell," had analyzed HCE as the "male figure" of *Finnegans Wake*, the one who, I quote, "plays the parts of father, lover, builder, sinner, 'Allmen'. . . ."[126]

On the father's side, this time, she says. She takes sides with the father and not with the living mother now. But how can one dissociate the two bodies and why in the end, and in the beginning, this insistence on the side [*côté*]—or on the rib [*côte*]? No doubt you have already been thinking about it for a long time, I am therefore coming back too quickly and too late to what you could hold to be the "agelessness" of a genesis, of the origin and of the genealogy of genius.[127] Such "agelessness" cannot possibly grow old, and it is never too late to talk about what the mother's side or the father's side may still mean, where in the end their conjoined, even conjugal, omnipotence knows that it watches, undissociated, like a single body in two bodies over a third body. Where does Eve, her primeval mother, omnipotent and all-living—on whose side I am, she says—come from? According to a certain narrative, which henceforth will no longer be so fictional, Eve comes from the rib or from the side of a certain earthling, of a certain earth-man, *Adam le glébeux* [dust-bound Adam], as Chouraqui translates. Now Georges, as his name indicates, is also an earth-man, a son of the earth, an elemental son, he is near the land that he works, the earth that he turns over and to which he eventually returns. And if she is born, elementally, from Adam and Eve, that is to say, primevally from Eve who primarily comes from Adam as from the side of his rib, she takes after both [*tient des deux*] but is no more held [*pas plus tenue*] to them than Eve herself. For if Eve is a part, via the rib, of the whole from which she is detached, she is indeed *detached* from it. You cannot imagine how detached Eve is, detached as a part of, as if apart from him, a part of and apart from the whole. Like Eve, she is also detached, she knows how to detach herself from what she is detached from, and this is the substitution, the art of detachment; for Eve knows how to expose herself to temptation, but she is no more exposed than this Adam, the Georges whose rib and side will have suffered so much, vulnerable as they were, generous, given, given over, given up, exposed to premature death as much as to birth, to what came from him but also apart from him, departed from him.

Where was I? Yes, the manuscript of this *Prénom de Dieu*. So I go on holiday, to a house in the country, with this text that had neither a name nor a forename yet. And I ask myself what happened to me, which still remains indescribable to me today: a mixture of revelation and incomprehension, an avid reading but one unable to recognize what it was reading here. What is happening here, I said to myself without hearing myself say so, without knowing whether I was hearing myself or implying it [*sans m'entendre à entendre si je sous-entends*]: What on earth is happening here? What is brought into the world and into literature, etc.? Or "What is happening to me here?"; "What am I going to do with this?"; "What on earth is this type, this new type of raving and sublime autobiography?"; "Who is this?"; "What is it that she wants?" I must have experienced a double feeling: enchanted admiration, quasi-religious fright (what on earth is happening here?), like someone who, walking alone in a desert of despairing [*désespérance*] (this feeling that was and still remains mine but which I bore and suffered from with more difficulty back then), sees a sort of miracle suddenly appear, which he is afraid of mistaking for a mirage, which he feels the desire to both recognize/reconnoitre by getting near it and flee from by warding it off. By denying and avoiding it. A multiple desire, then: either to move on or to make-let it come, see it coming—or else to follow and accompany an unpredictable birth. And how to speak about that? How not to speak about that? I have always hesitated and retreated before the language of "natural" force, which I am often tempted to turn toward her, as when one speaks of elemental genius, of "natural force," or of "force of nature": volcano, torrent, tidal surge, storm, the frenzy of that which sweeps everything away. I hesitate rather between the brutality of this naturalist, genealogist, or genetic language—which is also a denial, a refusal to understand and read—

and the secret murmur of a language of "fine silence." As is said in Kings (I, 19:12) about an almighty but almost inaudible God who addresses Elijah in a light, airy voice, beyond the majestic and spectacular attributes of his sovereignty.[128]

And while ceaselessly asking myself what kind of new species, what unique individual of a new unclassifiable species of literary animal or poetic prose I was dealing with, I no doubt began worrying. I believe I said to myself, some thirty-five years ago, identifying with her while separating myself from her, resolutely keeping at a distance: that one is mad, they will never read or "one will never read," one will never accept, one will never legitimize this, she does not see that a real resistance will be organized, or else it will take the work of generations, she goes too fast and with too much force, she lives too fast,[129] one must not accelerate all of a sudden, like that. She does not see the obstacle toward which she is rushing. She is not a good enough sociologist of the literary milieu in Paris. I was only half mistaken. I do not remember what I told her, back then, no doubt the truth of what I thought, as always, but probably by putting it somewhat more tactfully. I even wrote the "blurb" on the back cover of the book, from which the publisher only kept a few lines but whose original I have just found again among my papers. I have got it here; I find it with a smile, concerning her or myself, almost somnambulistic in its fore-sight.

When I began preparing for this session, my intention was to give you a detailed rereading of this first book. Naturally the premises since this morning—for these were only premises for this return to God's forename—left me no time for that. Not even the time necessary to tell you at least something about what had taken my breath away on the first reading: the speed, the transgressive force, the mighty power of truth of the phantasm, her relentless analysis, the serious play with the multiple sexual identities of who says "I," an I that is often masculine, as in the first short stories (*L'Outre vide, La Manche, La Lyre*) or as in *La Baleine de Jonas,* which begins thus:

My name is Jonah. Jonah is my family's name, it has been handed down to me by the women. My father calls me "Georges" like him. Georges and also Samuel, and also "my son."[130]

Besides, all the *ors* in Georges and all the words bearing the golden letters *or* [*tous les mots en or*] already shine and rustle in *Le Prénom de Dieu*. A masculine figure of the subject as well, for example in the short story called *Le Successeur*, whose "I" also speaks like a son. Among other things, he says those words that I would have liked to reinscribe within their own movement:

I am ghostly. . . . I would say: "Life is long," and sometimes I say: "We will gather, later." Later. Late is a name for death. . . . I would only ever love death.[131]

So it is a son-man who speaks. He also says "*I died*," and further:

I was stuck. I was my father's subject, it was so. I would have to die to myself and live as a king. . . . I decided I should have two names, mine and the one that my mother used to give me at night . . . [132]

Or else:

I had three warning dreams:
One was that my father loved me and that I was the third person.[133]

This third person haunts her whole work, like the "third name" in *La Baleine de Jonas* or *Le Troisième Corps* (1970). Besides, if one wanted retrospectively to read beforehand all the future perfects of the books to come in this firstborn book (which may always be done but which can or must never be done, each book to come remaining a beginning irreducible to its homonymous past), well, one could point out that in the second of the three dreams announced, the son says he is "the happy rival of my father," and he, the third dreamed person, declares, "I was always *there*." "There" [*là*] is underlined and in italics, this *being-there* of the son, a third person that is not a *Dasein* for death, thus announcing the titles of two books at least, *La* (1979) and *Illa* (1980). I would have liked to reread, in truth read this book at last for the first time and discover in it before you, without any teleological illusion or retrospection, without saying "it is already there," all that inaugurates as well as prefigures the enchanting chant of the *live-ance* of life [vivement *de la vie*], of speed [*vitesse*], of spectral and phantasmatic vision through the experience of blinding, etc.. One should henceforth, as I have done already, use the word *vivement* as a verbal noun rather than as an adverb: one would say *le vivement* [the live-ance], *le vivier du vivement* [the life-pool of the live-ance]. An example of this teleological temptation, which I wish to avoid among so many others, would be the reemergence, more than thirty-five years later, of Jonah's whale as one reads the beginning [*ouverture*] of *OR* (as one would speak about the reading [*ouverture*] of a will). One can read the following in *OR*:

> Until my brother like Jonah's tired whale enters my study and re-gurgitates a perfectly dry package: take this, here's your Jonah.[134]

It will have taken thirty-five years of her own entire work, of her submerged work, for the brother to spit it out. Instead of following these calls or recalls, for which we have no time left and for which you do not need me, I prefer to rush toward the end, toward the next to last end. Which next to last end? That of this interminable discourse, of course, to which you will have listened with a grace for which I would never know how to repay you; and then the next to last end of *Le Prénom de Dieu*, since I am only going to quote from its next to last short story, *La Baleine de Jonas*, precisely, but above all that of a next to last detour, idle, enchanted, dreamed by a garden, a childhood paradise—a garden for an offering. The offering comes from her, yet again, rather than her being on the receiving end, and from *Illa*, which I have just named. In this garden of offering, we are going to meet C. We are going to follow C, and C its double.

In the memory of our common childhood, and although we never went there together, note that it is a blessed garden. If we have never been there together yet, we have often talked about it smiling, in a tone of what I myself call my *nostalgeria*[135] and she her *algeriance*.[136] And besides, in her book with Mireille Calle-Gruber, to whom we owe so much, *Photos de racines*, more precisely in her "Inter Views" with Mireille, a page is entitled "We Are of the Same Garden."[137] It is a page on which in fact she speaks better than I would ever have done myself of our respective experience, each of us in our own way, of life death. "We are of the same garden," she says without naming this garden on this page then. Everything leads me to guess that it is in Algiers, not far from the sea, very near the shore, a big botanical garden whose avenues are lined with all the living trees of the world to which the heaven and earth of our country can offer their hospitality. This Garden has a name dear to all the inhabitants of Algiers: the Jardin d'Essais. Now as I was rereading *Illa* these last days, always prey to forget-reading [*oublire*], I came upon this garden again whose name is illegible to whoever does not, on their side, share her secret.[138] And mine. The metamorphosis or the metaphrase itself, as untranslatable as a proper noun, returns to the origin of being, to the sudden emergence of the "it is [*c'est*]" and of the *Esse*. This song for the Jardin d'Essais maintains its inspiration over some ten pages. I can only evoke a few notes in C, in passages where, as you are going to hear, she also names our untranslatable "prememories." First, for instance:

> As long as I was looking for the name of the garden among names, I could not find it. **I tried and tried [j'essayai et j'essayai]**, I invented a whole garden of names without **success**. In the end I went to the real garden to ask him what he was called. And as soon as I was in the main avenue, the name was **there,—in-the-jardin-des-c'est—** where it **had-always-been**, in the garden, in the whole big, cool, and wild garden, it was planted **there**, an eloquent motive, and the whole garden evoked at the same time was contained in the name, which deployed itself fully above its own ground, still as strangely alien, pronounceable, inappropriable, **untranslatable**. There are names that allow themselves to be remembered only at the place where they derive their meaning. Where they have taken root in our prememories.[139]

A little later, this earthly paradise of being becomes the *jardin* *d'*Esse, the animals and the languages of this paradise receive the most beautiful hymn worthy of their names. One should reread it all, including the hymn of *all* the earth, of all her earth, which is all for the moment [*toute à l'heure*], of the all-panic of her earth, the hymn to the *panther* or *pant-earth* [panthère]. From the depths of what she calls "hymnic times," the name "panther" suddenly emerges, and she says:

> The musical etymology of the panther is always present in each of its bounds. Apart from the elephone, the panther is one of the few animals with a verbal origin.[140]

That the "it is" preoccupies her, that is to say, the answer to the question "what is it?" which she sometimes writes in a single word, like a noun, and that this preoccupation is carried to the point of impatience is something you would find evidenced in *Messie*—the literality of whose writing, moreover, is often given over to the lexicon of animal might, of life, speed, and vision. In one of her numerous great animal autobiographies, she then confesses:

> Now any Whatis [*Questceque*] presents itself to my consciousness like a most **powerful** specter, which first confiscates all the messages of the senses from me . . . [141]

After the next to last of these next to last detours, here is the next to last one, via the next to last short story of *Le Prénom de Dieu*. I am getting there, as if I wanted to be forgiven, as if I had to be forgiven. By you and by her. What? Forgetreading and betrayal—of which I will only take one example, the latest. Ever since I have known her, I have read her and I keep forgetting that she writes, and I forget what she writes. This forgetting is not a forgetting like any other; it is elemental, I probably live on it. Her work for me will remain for life like what I have already forgotten a priori: I forget it as naturally as I breathe. And not only as one forgets those canonical texts where one can find everything, like Shakespeare or the Bible, the Gospels, the genuine or spurious apocalypses, and Joyce, Blanchot, Kafka, and so many others, all those men and women who have already said everything in the past. No, this time, it would be an *all is well said* [tout est bien dit] or *benedictum* and just as soon forgotten but *an all is well said* of a moment ago [d'un tout est bien dit *de tout à l'heure*] as well as *contemporaneous*, living beside me and in the process of continuing. That is grace. I find my way again by forgetting, and I have the feeling that I will be forgiven . . .

As if she had given me permission to forget, as if I were giving myself permission. Then I am no longer ashamed to confess: you know, I had forgotten you had already written that too. I believe I told her more than once. I act as if I could no longer know who wrote that first [*la première*]. And as if I left unresolved the question: who will ever know? And yet, in order to get the measure of how outrageous what I am saying here really is, you must know how little the things the two of us [*l'une et l'autre*] write resemble one another, especially when we write each other ourselves [*nous nous écrivons*] autobiographically:[142] you must admit that it is difficult to imagine anything more different, difficult to imagine writings, ways, manners, gestures, rhythms, languages, lives of writing, and simply lives that are more heterogeneous, more dissimilar, more distant from each other and on both sides. And families of texts each more foreign to each other. Whereas (or because) everything we write, she and I, remains strictly autobiographical, as they say. We only ever write ourselves, on ourselves. *Nous* nous *écrivons*. Translate: we write to each other, she and I have written each other a lot. But what you have just translated thus (we have written each other a lot) remains absolutely untranslatable (therefore readable, unreadable). In another language you could not leave this indecisive statement as it is, in its undecidable state, between "us," between the two "us" who say to each other "we have written ourselves a lot" and "we have written each other a lot" (ourselves for ourselves or the one to the other), and this indecision between two homonyms is not a game. It is so serious that it remains undecidable for me. An absolute difference, which can come to the same thing around here. Between us, there is language. To be revived. To kindle without animosity. It is the truth: there are cases when, when two write, one no longer knows whether they write (to) each other or themselves [*s'ils s'écrivent ou s'ils s'écrivent*], and whether a lot covers all or part of the homonymy.

Here is the latest example, then. In *Le Prénom de Dieu*, it will not be *Anagramme*, the last short story, whose first voice announces: "It will be the next to last day of the month," and in which you would find, with all the ghosts to come, a poem for which I cannot find a match here and which I urge you to read, a poem on the afterlife of the living dead, the letters and the name of Death, dream, and knowledge, and which signs in "seeing that every life is nothing but what I bring alive into the world, and death that which I refused as a mortal." This poem ends thus (these are the last words of the book):

> Then I knew that my faithfulness was rewarded, I knew that I had had my next to last day, and I understood that the next to last day was nothing but the last, or the last one the first of all eternity. And everything had already been said long ago.[143]

In *La Baleine de Jonas*, the next to last short story of *Le Prénom de Dieu*, which one should also devour and incorporate again whole, knowledge is measured against the awareness of a heritage, against a duty, an obligation to inherit: "My father had had it before me and had bequeathed it to me on his death," the voice says, and toward the end, I cut: "I knew that I had to inherit. . . ."

To inherit what? Wait a bit if you do not have the book in mind.

It so happens that, about two years ago, in a so-called autobiographical text entitled *Un Ver à soie*, I devoted a long tender meditation to my tallith, among other things, to this prayer shawl, this white silk veil that my grandfather had given to me. In this text I talk of benediction and of death, of the white tallith that my father had borrowed from me and of the one in which he had been shrouded, as is the custom. But let us leave my text aside. You can easily imagine that if I knew or if I recalled at that moment that there was a text by Hélène Cixous on the tallith, I would have done one of two things, believe me: either I would have abstained from speaking about mine or else I would have honestly referred to hers, all the more so since *Un Ver à soie* also talks about Hélène Cixous and about another of her texts, *Savoir*. And all the more so, especially, since my real tallith remains fully mine, in life, my father too, and so our respective stories as irreducible the one to the other as possible. To each his own father and to each his own mother.[144] The real story of my tallith, my autobiographical an-amnesis, as spontaneous as possible, with all that hangs by its silk threads, all that did not need her in any way, apparently, did not need her own memory and even less what she could have written about it.

This remains true but naturally I was in a state of absolute for-getreading, and just these past weeks, as I was rereading *La Bale-ine de Jonas*, which I must have, should have met some thirty-five years ago, well, I found, found again where I had not found it, a tallith, which has no reason to be jealous of mine which has every reason to be jealous of it. An entirely other tallith, sewn [*cousu*] entirely otherwise, but also related [*cousin*] to mine.

One can of course calculate a thousand historical probabilities in order to foresee this crossing. Still, the feeling of magical telepa-thy remains intact. And supernatural.

Do not forget—and that is also a theme in my *Ver à soie*—the daughters do not wear a tallith. The daughters, the women, the mothers, the sisters cannot and must not. They have no right to it.

Whereas she does, when she signs—in the masculine. She takes it. She takes the right and takes it by surprise; she takes it in and changes it. Not in order to change talliths as easily as one changes one's mind or one's clothes, men's clothes,[145] but also to inherit it on her side, and draw the other out of death by the wisps of his tallith. Here again, one should reread everything, like the six hundred fringes, for a tallith has six hundred fringes, just as she has six hundred voices, plus the threads and knots of the tallith. I must tighten things up around the blind man (*La Baleine de Jonas already* said, if one can say "already," all that is said about blind-ness, thirty-five years later, in *Savoir*), and then around the breath and the specter—and around the father's inherited tallith. It is in a section of the short story entitled *Mon Remplaçant.* Here are a few sentences:

> . . . thinking I have no more eyes to see him, not knowing I am sole master of every gaze: not long ago, in order to satisfy his hunger for pomp, he sold me his right to see. I bought eyes from him, as in the old tales. . . . I whisper to him that I am the specter. . . . The blind man answers for me. . . . Inside [*dedans*] I set about working . . . and I contained the lost object, it was inside, and the inside was my being [you remember that *Dedans* was the title of the book that followed *Le Prénom de Dieu* in 1969 and rated highly [*à la cote*] when it was awarded the Prix Médicis ... —JD], I looked for the embroidered seal in it, the fringe of knotted silk, where the master had hidden my name. . . . I knew that the name was in the silk knots of the tallith, I need only have taken hold of it and God would have woven me and all silence would have become voice. My father had had it before me and had bequeathed it to me on his death. Draped in the signed fabric, I was playing at impersonating my father, my brothers, and me-yesterday or me-tomorrow, never myself because I did not love myself . . . [146]

The substitute [*remplaçant*], Narcissus the son or the brother, says he did not love himself.

And after pages on this strange impersonation by a daughter whom I set out to impersonate unknowingly, on which you could count the number of times the word *gorge* [throat, breast] (that of the whale, of course) occurs, you would discover, still on the side, two short treatises on the existence of God (to quote the subtitle of a book, *Beethoven à jamais ou l'existence de Dieu*, thirty years younger: 1993). Here is, on the next to last and last pages of *La Baleine de Jonas*, in *Le Prénom de Dieu*, God's forename, and again, already, a certain "I am on this side":

> What if I had always been God? And if God was my real name and if God was the shadow of my absence, and if he was the father of my death? What if he was the sun and I the moon? Or if he was the day and I the night? I dream him, he kills me, I drive him away, he pursues me, I am God, he is Jonah. Between us there is only the book left, and we read the same page in turn. When he is on **the other side of the book, I am on this side**. . . .

But God dreams us and in his dream He kills us and eats us; He encompasses us. His dream feeds on our billions of dreams. All dream so that God dreamexists [*rêvexiste*].[147]

"Dreamexists," she says, in one word: this concept of dreamexistence—for it is a concept—in a word tells everything; besides Eve's name, which it has in its voice, in its mouth, or in its jaws, it tells of her own way of existing, writing, and calling things into being from the mighty powers of dream. It says above all that God's existence is *proved* by dream, more effectively than by all the onto-theologico-philosophical proofs. A proof for, but, or now [*or*], it is a dream existence not only because God dreams, because he is dream, because we ineluctably dream the existence of God, because this existence dreams *itself*, but because the pleading power of *might*, at the infinite speed of which there is no more difference or lag between virtuality and actuality, between the desire of the phantasm and reality, between dream and reality, is the event that makes things happen in a dream. As in a dream. The phantasm is, like faith, the best proof of God's existence, the only one in truth. And one must draw all the consequences from this.

I am again skipping, and after a big blank, from one paragraph to the next, here is the other side:

> . . . Thus spoke my Master. When he had finished speaking, I knew it was time henceforth for him to keep silent [*qu'il se tût*, spelled *t-û-t*, not *qu'il se tue* [for him to kill himself]! Or is it [*mais si*]?—JD], I knew I had to inherit his shawl.
> I wrapped myself in silk; sat in front of God's mouth, with the book opened in front of me, I began a roll call of my brothers' names. I thought: "Against Him, it is harpoons we need." And if I am still there, with the list of Jonahs [plural: it is a lineage of substitutes—JD] in front of me, it is written that I am; seated on the other side of the beginning, I am dead, I stay.[148]

It is the end, the end of the short story [*nouvelle*], what happens in/to the end and whose news [*nouvelle*] is the story.

Epilogue

We are not going to argue over a tallith, nor especially over the shawl of the Master, for whom she knows that "it was time to keep silent" and from whom every one of us would inherit on their sides.

I would like to give mine to her as a present, since, as she said to me the other day, she seems to have forgotten hers.

But just imagine the scene of giving her a tallith she already has, even in a garden of innocence; that would run the risk of still resembling a claim for ownership in an inheritance lawsuit.

Above all, since the inheritance of the tallith can only be received by a son or a brother, it would be like giving to him and not to her, even if she knows how to say "*Illa.*"[149]

Then, if I gave the tallith to her, if she had it, whereas she already had it and, like me, had forgotten it, if I gave it back to her, we would still be arguing.

Now I am ready to argue over everything, to argue with her over everything, except a tallith.

I argue with her all the time, I begin again all the time, I told you so when I began.

Between her and me, it is as if it were a question of life and death. Death would be on my side and life on hers.

I would attempt to be convinced of life by her, preparing myself to receive grace instead of the coup de grâce, but I am and remain for life *convaincu de mort* (both *convicted* and *convinced* of death); *convicted,* that is to say at fault and accused, found guilty, imprisoned or jailed after a verdict, here a death sentence, but also *convinced,* convinced by the truth of death, of a true speech (*veridictum*), of a verdict as regards death. She, on her Side [*de son Côté, avec un grand C*], it is [*c'est*] for life she is convinced of life for life.

Death counts for her, certainly, on every page, but she herself does not count. For me, death counts, it counts, and my days, my hours, and my seconds are numbered.

It is as if [*si*] she said: "We're not going to die"; "Yes we are [*mais si*]," I would answer. She knows I tell the truth, I know she tells the truth. Now evidently we say the opposite, how is that possible? Who is dreaming in all this evidence?

The thing is, I just cannot believe her, as far as life death is concerned, from one side to the other. I just cannot believe her, that is to say: I can only manage to believe her, I only manage to believe her when she speaks in the subjunctive.

That's how it is, and it will be I believe like that up to the end, comprehensively [*comprise*]. Yes, comprehensively. Up to the end, supposing that she ever be comprehended [*comprise*], in the end.

Up to the end but, precisely, that will be the end.

Notes

Translator's Preface

1. A literal translation of the original title, *H.C. pour la vie, c'est à dire . . .* , was felt to be the most satisfactory way of doing justice to the subtle polysemy of its wording, spelling, and syntax, as well as its aural effects. The reader may wish to hear *c'est pour la vie* (that is for life), especially since Derrida often plays on the near-homophony between the letter *C* and *c'est* in French, as well as understand *c'est à dire*, usually hyphenated throughout to mean "that is to say"—the book is an endless rebeginning of itself in other words—also as an injunction: that is/ needs to be said.

2. "Hélène has a genius for making the language speak, down to the most familiar idiom, the place where it seems to be crawling with secrets which give way to thought" (Derrida's foreword to *The Hélène Cixous Reader*, ed. Susan Sellers, preface by Hélène Cixous and Jacques Derrida [London: Routledge, 1994], p. vii).

H.C. for Life, That Is to Say . . .

1. There seemed no better way of rendering this iterative *puisse* than to bring back to life this slightly archaic construction, "Would that I might," which makes it possible to keep Derrida's constant structural coupling of the subjunctive "might" [*puisse*], including as an invented, nominalized form (*le "puisse," la "puisse"*), with the noun "might" [*puissance*] wherever appropriate. Where "might" was too awkward lexically

or syntactically, "mighty power" or, more simply, "power" was used instead, often with the French in square brackets.—Trans.

2. Derrida refers to Hélène Cixous, *La* (Paris: Gallimard, 1976; Des Femmes, 1979), whose homophony with *là* ("there," but often meaning "here" in English), he will take up later. (Unless otherwise indicated, all the works referenced in the notes are by Hélène Cixous.)—Trans.

3. This versatile idiomatic phrase, which can also refer to "a moment ago," i.e., in the past, will be repeated time and again, often in conjunction with other temporal variations—and occasionally declined into *tout(e) à l'heure* (literally, "all for the hour"). We have indicated the most obviously thematicized temporal markers in square brackets in order to draw the reader's attention to the continuity of Derrida's reflection on or around the French *heure*, "hour," often converted to "moment" here.—Trans.

4. The scene that follows is quoted and retold by Hélène Cixous herself in *Portrait de Jacques Derrida en Jeune Saint Juif* (Paris: Galilée, 2001), p. 13 (*Portrait of Jacques Derrida as a Young Jewish Saint*, trans. Beverley Bie Brahic (New York: Columbia University Press, 2004), pp. 5–6; translation modified).—Trans.

5. Derrida's dense humorous development brings together *par ici* ("this way," "through here," and, in most other contexts, "[around] here"), *parousie*, and the name of the conference venue, *Cerisy*, as well as, in the next paragraph, *parricide*—*par ici* sounding like a half-pronounced *parricide* in French, therefore a *quasi*-parricide or a parricide *en comme si* (French *comme si* = Latin *quasi*: as if).—Trans.

6. Both *si* (if, yes)—with the later adjunction of the musical note B (*en si ou en comme si*)—and "six" already start articulating the family name *Cixous*, whose initial *C*, almost pronounced like *c'est* (this is), will be extensively glossed later on.—Trans.

7. *Le Prénom de Dieu* (Paris: Grasset, 1967).

8. *Les Commencements* (Paris: Grasset, 1970; Des Femmes, 1999).

9. The title of Cixous's novel *OR, les lettres de mon père* (Paris: Des Femmes, 1997), to which Derrida alludes here, contains another homophony: the conjunction *or*, "now" (omitted in English in the minor premise of a syllogism; cf. p. 6 *supra*), and the noun *or*, "gold," with, in this particular sentence, the added aural effect *or, d'elle-même*, suggesting *hors d'elle*, "beside herself."—Trans.

10. Derrida makes the untranslatable ambiguity of Cixous's *mes proches morts* explicit by referring to the English equivalents, "dead ones"

and "deaths." For a discussion of the various semantic layers, see Eric Prenowitz, "Nearly Reading Hélène Cixous: the 'Equivocal Vocation' of Translation," in *Joyful Babel: Translating Hélène Cixous*, ed. Myriam Diocaretz and Marta Segarra (Amsterdam: Rodopi, 2004), pp. 47–60.—Trans.

11. *OR, les lettres de mon père*, p. 199.

12. *L'Histoire (qu'on ne connaîtra jamais)* (Paris: Des Femmes, 1994).

13. We wish to keep Derrida's crucial distinction, often reiterated in his texts of the last decade, between *futur* (future) and *avenir*, which is always to come [*à venir*], hence "future-to-come."—Trans.

14. *Derrenier, dé-renier* (and later, *de-renier*; cf. p. 116 *infra*), and *déreniement* combine *dernier, dernièrement* ("last," "lastly," hence "rear"), *dénier* ("to deny"), and *renier* or *reniement* ("to disown," often translated as "to renege" in order to make available the play on "re(ar)-negation" and "de-negation" (*dénégation*, "denial") whenever appropriate.—Trans.

15. "*Je est un autre*" is Arthur Rimbaud's celebrated exclamation in a letter to Paul Demeny, dated May 15, 1871 (*Oeuvres complètes*, ed. Antoine Adam [Paris: Gallimard, 1972], p. 250).—Trans.

16. Cf. *Le Prénom de Dieu*. "Prenamed" (from "prename": forename, first name) is chosen here to capture some of Derrida's near-etymological play on a *prénom* being barely a name since it comes "initially," before a (proper) name.—Trans.

17. One of Derrida's motifs throughout the book, *du côté de . . .*, is an obvious reference to Marcel Proust's *Du Côté de chez Swann*, translated into English as *Swann's Way*. Of all the French *côtés*, this sense of "direction" is the one that simply cannot be forced into English as a "side," hence "down her way" here, which conveys some of the literary allusion.—Trans.

18. *Les Commencements* (Paris: Grasset, 1970), p. 177 (Des Femmes, 1999, p. 160, hereafter given in brackets).

19. Derrida uses the word "quote" in the original, together with the French equivalent *cite*, and will do so on several other occasions. In fact Derrida often resorts to English or anglicized words instead of, or alongside, the French, and we have felt the need to indicate the most thematically relevant occurrences in square brackets.—Trans.

20. *Messie* (Paris: Des Femmes, 1996), p. 102. The title sounds almost like *mais si*, a recurrent tag in Derrida's text that has sometimes been given in square brackets because there is no single possible translation.—Trans.

21. Derrida plays on the humorous colloquialism "*je mens comme je respire*," (literally) I lie the way I breathe, i.e., I am a born liar (compare also with "I forget it as naturally as I breathe," p. 152)—or even *elle ment comme elle respire*—in a passage where he introduces the playful parsing of *élé-ment* (pronounced almost like *elle ment*) and *événe-ment*, the latter occurring in an excerpt from Cixous's *Les Commencements* discussed below (cf. n. 30 *infra*).—Trans.

22. "To reread, that is to say read, that is to say resurrect-erase that is to say *forgetread* [oublire]" (*OR, les lettres de mon père*, p. 16; cited p. 98, with the page wrongly identified as p. 17 in the original).—Trans.

23. A *décade* is the word traditionally used for a ten-day conference held at Cerisy-la-Salle. This specific meaning dates back to the Republican calendar introduced during the French Revolution, and here Derrida deliberately plays on the ambiguity with the English translation for *décennie*: a ten-year period.—Trans.

24. *Jours de l'an* (Paris: Des Femmes, 1990), p. 154 [*FirstDays of the Year*, trans. Catherine A. F. Gillivray (Minneapolis: University of Minnesota Press, 1998), p. 102; translation slightly modified]. (The bold type that follows is not in the text, of course.)

25. *OR, les lettres de mon père*, p. 37.

26. *Numéro pair bis* (which sounds like *père bis*; cf. p. 25 *supra*): 10A would be an equivalent example.—Trans.

27. *Les Commencements*, p. 33 (p. 21).

28. *En si et en là*: Derrida's praise of the aurality/orality of Cixous's writing is matched by several tonal allusions via the first syllable of her name, pronounced like *si* (the note B), and the homophony of *la* (A) in the sol-fa scale with the title of one of her books, but also with *là (there)*. Cixous herself has further brought out this musical vein in her retelling of the "primal scene" of their missed encounter by playing on the homophony in French between Derrida's *dos* (back) and *do* (the note C; see n. 4 *supra*).—Trans.

29. *Les Commencements*, pp. 35–36 (pp. 23–24).

30. As Derrida's subsequent development makes clear, the French *Ève ne ment* (Eve does not lie) sounds like *événement*, the French word for "event," hence the translation's slightly convoluted syntax, which is meant to spell out the sequence of letters "**even t**ell."—Trans.

31. *Les Commencements*, p. 84 (p. 69).

32. In fact, *tempus* is neuter in the singular, despite the *-us* ending, which sounds like the familiar marker of masculine nouns in Latin.—Trans.

33. *Les Commencements*, p. 39 (p. 27).

34. *Les Commencements*, p. 40 (p. 28).

35. *OR, les lettres de mon père*, p. 20.

36. *OR, les lettres de mon père*, pp. 190–91.

37. *Jours de l'an*, p. 173 [*FirstDays of the Year*, p. 115; translations modified].

38. This is already a quotation from *Jours de l'an*, p. 174 [*FirstDays of the Year*, p. 116], just before the following excerpt (translation modified).—Trans.

39. *Jours de l'an*, p. 174 [*FirstDays of the Year*, p. 116; translation modified].

40. *Jours de l'an.*, pp. 176–77 [*FirstDays of the Year*, pp. 117–18; translation modified].

41. *Jours de l'an*, p. 177 [*FirstDays of the Year*, p. 118 (translation modified)].

42. *Déesse*, "goddess," is pronounced like the two letters D.S., a literal homophony consonant with Derrida's play on H.C.'s initials throughout, and which Roland Barthes had made popular in his analysis of the generational symbol of "The New Citroën" in *Mythologies*, trans. Annette Lavers (London: Vintage, 1993), pp. 88–90. But "the female first name of God" also suggests that D.S. might be a punning acronym for *différence sexuelle*, which Cixous uses for e.g. in "Contes de la Différence Sexuelle," in *Lectures de la différence sexuelle*, ed. Mara Negrón (Paris: Des Femmes, 1994), p. 35.—Trans.

43. *Jours de l'an*, p. 178 [*FirstDays of the Year*, p. 118 (translation modified)]. In this instance, we resorted to decapitalizing May in English in order to render the quirk of the French: *may*, instead of *mai*.—Trans.

44. *Jours de l'an*, p. 178 [*FirstDays of the Year*, pp. 118–19 (translation modified)].

45. Cixous's lecture for the 1992 *décade*, "Quelle heure est-il ou La porte (celle qu'on ne passe pas)," began thus: "The first time I saw Jacques Derrida (it must have been in 1962), he was walking [...] along a mountain's crest." In *Le Passage des frontières: Autour du travail de Jacques Derrida* (Paris: Galilée, 1994), p. 83; "What is it o'clock? or The door (we never enter)," trans. Catherine A. F. MacGillivray, in Hélène Cixous, *Stigmata: Escaping Texts* (London: Routledge, 1998), p. 57.—Trans.

46. *OR, les lettres de mon père*, pp. 139ff.

47. I refer you to the admirable "Petrarca et le pardon," by Giuseppe Motta, *Rivista di estetica* 9, n.s., (1998).

48. *Jours de l'an*, pp. 18ff [*FirstDays of the Year*, pp. 12ff].

49. *OR, les lettres de mon père*, p. 142 (emphases mine, of course).

50. *Les Commencements*, p. 57 (p. 44) (my emphasis).

51. *Jours de l'an*, pp. 193–95 [*FirstDays of the Year*, pp. 130–31].

52. Literally "axe," but "hatchet" has been silently substituted in the following excerpts from *FirstDays of the Year* in order to render the thematic cogency of Derrida's argument involving the letter *H*, similarly pronounced, and, in Cixous's text, an implicit allusion to the semiproverbial phrase *l'Histoire avec sa grande hache* (History with its big axe / capital *H*). See also p. 105.—Trans.

53. *Jours de l'an*, p. 193 [*FirstDays of the Year*, p. 130; translation modified].

54. *Beethoven à jamais ou l'existence de Dieu* (Paris: Des Femmes, 1993), p. 226.

55. *Beethoven à jamais ou l'existence de Dieu*, p. 233.

56. *Beethoven à jamais ou l'existence de Dieu*, p. 210. (Unless otherwise indicated, all the emphases are mine.)

57. *Beethoven à jamais ou l'existence de Dieu*, pp. 214–15.

58. This is one of several instances where Derrida deliberately juxtaposes the masculine grammatical gender (unavailable in English) of *auteur* with the feminine personal pronoun referring to Cixous, who is later explicitly referred to as a "man of the theater" and a "man of action" within a "feminist" context emphasizing her monumental achievements.—Trans.

59. An allusion to a novel by Cixous bearing this title (Paris: Denoël, 1973; Des Femmes, 1999).—Trans.

60. *Beethoven à jamais ou l'existence de Dieu*, p. 211.

61. *Memoirs of the Blind: The Self-Portrait and Other Ruins*, trans. Pascale-Anne Brault and Michael Naas (Chicago: University of Chicago Press, 1993).

62. "Savoir," in Hélène Cixous and Jacques Derrida, *Veils*, trans. Geoffrey Bennington (Stanford, CA: Stanford University Press, 2001), pp. 1–16.

63. *Jours de l'an*, pp. 155–56 [*FirstDays of the Year*, p. 103].

64. *Et chante la hantise*: Derrida's development implicitly plays on the homophony between *champs* (fields) and *chants* (songs).—Trans.

65. A more literal double translation—which will be more appropriate in subsequent, "critical" contexts—could be: I saw letters / I live on letters (or even literature).—Trans.

66. *OR, les lettres de mon père*, pp. 186–87. I had noted the work of the letter V in her texts (cf. "Un ver à soie," in H. Cixous and J. Derrida, *Voiles* [Paris: Galilée, 1999]) ["A Silkworm of One's Own," in *Veils*, pp. 17–92].

67. The quasi-neologism *arrivant* was first introduced and discussed in *Aporias*, trans. Thomas Dutoit (Stanford, CA: Stanford University Press, 1993), esp. p. 33; in n. 14 (p. 86). Derrida adds that he recalled after the fact that Cixous had used the term earlier in her works.—Trans.

68. *OR, les lettres de mon père*, pp. 186–87.

69. *En puissance:* usually translated as "potentially" or, more philo-sophically, "in potentiality," this phrase has an added twist of difficulty on account of the conceptual revitalization of *puissance* throughout. We have therefore resorted to grading our translations according to the context as well as the syntactico-semantic environment, hence a more empowered "in might" here, in keeping with *mighting*, since *en puis-sance* is explicitly envisaged beyond the opposition between act(uality) and potentiality. The reader should likewise feel empowered by Derrida's pliable idiom, used to capture the liberating effects of Cixous's prose, to modulate our resigned choice of "in potentiality" in most cases with "might" and, in this work praising Cixous's art of replacement, invent substitute constructs, such as "in mighty potentiality" or "in potential might," etc.—Trans.

70. I confess that I had not yet read, by the time of Cerisy, the mag-nificent text that Mireille Calle-Gruber devotes to "La vision prise de vi-tesse par l'écriture, à propos de *La Fiancée juive*, d'Hélène Cixous" (*Lit-térature* 103 [October 1996]: 79–93). I do not know a more lucid analysis of the "race" of a writing that "functions like a marvelous gearbox," of its "time without time" and of the "magnets" of these "magnetic fields" where the writing is "challenged: to race faster than itself."

71. *Jours de l'an*, p. 179 [*FirstDays of the Year*, p. 119].

72. Derrida had already developed this point in "Fourmis," in *Lec-tures de la différence sexuelle*, pp. 80–81, 97, and will return to it in *Ge-nèses, généalogies, genres et le génie: Les secrets de l'archive* (Paris: Galilée, 2003), p. 49ff.—Trans.

73. *Entre l'écriture* (Paris: Des Femmes, 1986) is the title of one of Cixous's collections of critical essays; *Coming to Writing and Other Es-says*, ed. Deborah Jenson, trans. Sarah Cornell et al. (Cambridge, Mass: Harvard University Press, 1991).—Trans.

74. " . . . *qui s'entend à faire arriver l'adresse même.*" Another transla-

tion could be: " . . . which can be heard when it makes the address itself arrive." Derrida will return on several occasions to the thematic link, half-articulated before, between knowing, aurality (hearing), and understanding in the French verb *entendre, s'entendre à.*—Trans.

75. *OR, les lettres de mon père*, pp. 20–21.

76. Derrida subsequently develops the etymological ties in the French *raccorder* (and later *s'accorder*) between *corde* ("chord," but also "cord," "rope," from Latin *chorda*), the heart (French *coeur*, from Latin *cor, cordis*), and accord, to which the translation has resorted occasionally.—Trans.

77. *Croisées d'une oeuvre* (Crossroads of an Oeuvre) was the title chosen for the *décade* on Hélène Cixous at which this lecture was first given. Cf. p. 57 *supra.*—Trans.

78. The French phrase may be construed as a cross between *entre chien et loup* ("in the gloaming") and *comme chien et chat* ("like cat and dog," or here Cixous's female cat [*chatte*]).—Trans.

79. *OR, les lettres de mon père*, p. 88.

80. *OR, les lettres de mon père*, pp. 147–48. [The first half of this dense passage in "*or*" (*sort*: "goes out," "fate"; *mort*: "dead," "death") should be compared with the French original.—Trans.]

81. Cf. "Faith and Knowledge: the Two Sources of 'Religion' at the Limits of Reason Alone," trans. Samuel Weber, in *Religion*, ed. Jacques Derrida and Gianni Vattimo (London: Polity, 1998), pp. 1–78 (orig. Paris: Seuil, 1996). Weber's translations of the key "concepts" have been used as far as possible for the sake of consistency across translations.—Trans.

82. *OR, les lettres de mon père*, p. 21.

83. "A Silkworm of One's Own," in *Veils*, pp. 17–92.

84. This is one of several passages structured by Derrida's strategic use of gendered pronouns in French, here *elle*, which can refer either to animate or inanimate nouns.—Trans.

85. Prawns (*crevettes roses*), rather than shrimps (*crevettes grises*). We are grateful to Hélène Cixous for clarifying this instance of the intrusion of the real into the linguistic.—Trans.

86. Here Derrida refers in English to J. L. Austin's well-known *How to Do Things with Words* (Oxford: Clarendon Press, 1962), in which the American linguist introduced the notion of the performative, which Derrida subsequently discussed in "Signature, Event, Context" (in *Margins of Philosophy*, trans. Alan Bass [Chicago: University of Chicago Press, 1982], pp. 307–30).—Trans.

87. Derrida's (and Cixous's) versatile use of the French verb *faire*, especially in *faire un nom*, is more conspicuous from this point onward and has called for an equally flexible approach in the translation, with the French being given in square brackets whenever appropriate.—Trans.

88. Cf. n. 22 *supra*.

89. Derrida refers in English to Shelley's poem "The Triumph of Life," which had been chosen as the focus text for an illustrative collection of essays by "Yale deconstructionists," to which he contributed "Living On: Border Lines" (in Harold Bloom et al., *Deconstruction and Criticism* [London: Routledge and Kegan Paul, 1979], pp. 75–176).—Trans.

90. *OR, les lettres de mon père*, pp. 17–18 and ff. for subsequent quotations.

91. *Jours de l'an*, p. 217 ["An Ideal Story," in *FirstDays of the Year*, pp. 139–88; quotation p. 147].

92. *Anankè* (Paris: Des Femmes, 1979), p. 166.

93. *Anankè*, p. 170.

94. *Anankè*, p. 171.

95. *La Fiancée juive—de la tentation* (Paris: Des Femmes, 1995), pp. 17, 87.

96. *Beethoven à jamais ou l'existence de Dieu*, ch. 9: "La trahison," pp. 207–35.

97. *Jours de l'an*, pp. 126–27 [*FirstDays of the Year*, p. 83].

98. *Jours de l'an*, p. 48 [*FirstDays of the Year*, p. 32].

99. Derrida quotes in English Stephen Dedalus's famous definition of paternity in the "Scylla and Charybdis" chapter of James Joyce's *Ulysses*.—Trans.

100. An ironic allusion to the now semiproverbial opening of René Descartes's *Discourse on Method*.—Trans.

101. More precisely, Salomon Reinach's article "L'art et la magie," in *Cultes, Mythes et Religions*, vol. 1 (1905), pp. 125–36.—Trans.

102. The active principle in the verbal noun (see also *vivement*) is also to be heard in *puissance*: as it were, "might-ing" (an active principle combined with the potentiality of a subjunctive; cf. p. 70 and n. 69 *supra*), and is to be understood in the light of Derridean *différance, arrivance, aimance* (cf. *Politiques de l'amitié* [Paris: Galilée, 1994], p. 88) or, further in *H.C. pour la vie, mourance* and *désespérance*, as well as Cixous's *algériance* (cf. p. 151 *infra* and n. 136).—Trans.

103. *OR, les lettres de mon père*, p. 115.

104. Ovid, *Metamorphoses*, Book 3, trans. A. D. Melville, intro. and

notes by E. J. Kenney (Oxford: Oxford University Press, 1986), p. 62, ll. 379–83:

"'Anyone here?' and Echo answered 'Here!'
[Amazed he looked all round and,] raising his voice,
Called 'Come this way!' and Echo called 'This way!'"

105. Sigmund Freud, *Totem and Taboo*, in *Standard Edition of the Complete Psychological Works*, trans. and ed. James Strachey, vol. 13 (London: Hogarth Press: 1955), p. 93.

106. Here we have departed from the translation in the *Standard Edition* in order to stay closer to Derrida's wording.—Trans.

107. *Anankè*, p. 209.

108. *Les Commencements*, p. 39 (p. 27).

109. *Anankè*, p. 199.

110. See Max Weber, *Wissenschaft als Beruf* (Science as a Profession, 1922), especially the chapter entitled "*Rationalisierung, Fortschritt und Entzauberung der Welt.*"—Trans.

111. *L'Éloge d'Hélène*, in *Revue de poésie*, no. 90, "La parole dite," October 1964 [*Encomium of Helen*, intro., ed., trans. D. M. MacDowell (London: Duckworth; Bristol Classical Press, 1999), pp. 23, 25; the translation has been modified to reflect Derrida's use of the French version].

112. *OR, les lettres de mon père*, p. 186.

113. *OR, les lettres de mon père*, p. 25.

114. *OR, les lettres de mon père*, p. 186.

115. *OR, les lettres de mon père*, p. 198.

116. *OR, les lettres de mon père*, p. 81.

117. *L'Exil de James Joyce ou l'art du remplacement* (Paris: Grasset, 1968). The English version was simply called *The Exile of James Joyce*, trans. Sally A. J. Purcell (London: John Calder, 1976), which further adds to the difficulty of translating the French *remplacement* (as well as *remplacer*) consistently by "replacement," more readily suggestive of (taking the) place (of), rather than "substitution," throughout Derrida's book.—Trans.

118. *OR, les lettres de mon père*, pp. 189–91.

119. *OR, les lettres de mon père*, p. 192.

120. *OR, les lettres de mon père*, p. 197.

121. *Sans que j'y puisse rien; sans que je n'y puisse rien.* In certain constructions, the French language relies on the power of a formal negation without negative content called "expletive negation" to register the speaker's feeling that an action might ultimately not happen. French psy-

choanalyst Jacques Lacan was particularly adept at wielding the full force of this syntactically expendable particle to indicate how a speaker's unconscious might seek expression in the formal properties of the language of enunciation rather than at the level of manifest content.—Trans.

122. The acronym for Groupe d'Information sur les Prisons. This militant group was created in February 1971 (and dissolved in December 1972) in order to make public opinion aware of the growing importance of surveillance and punishment as hidden forces of social control and organization (to paraphrase Michel Foucault's inaugural words). Its main objectives were to mobilize against criminal records, denounce the social climate of mounting intolerance, including being prosecuted for one's beliefs, campaign against suicide in prison, etc.—Trans.

123. The term *sans papiers* was introduced in the mid 1990s following a successful vote on right-wing legislation intended to clamp down on clandestine or illegal immigration and give state authorities the right to expel from French territory immigrant workers and asylum seekers judged to be *en situation irrégulière*, i.e., without valid personal documents. The law was met with sharp resistance among left-wing sympathizers and intellectuals who demonstrated for the *régularisation* or legalization of individuals in this precarious situation.—Trans.

124. Established in 1994 on the initiative of Salman Rushdie in response to an appeal launched in 1993 by writers from around the world, following the upsurge in assassinations of writers in Algeria, its aim was to protect persecuted writers by offering an alternative network of asylum, residency, and solidarity.—Trans.

125. Antoinette Fouque founded the publishing house Des Femmes in 1973, five years after cofounding the famous militant French feminist party, the Mouvement de Libération des Femmes (MLF). The Théâtre du Soleil, directed by Ariane Mnouchkine, was set up in 1970 in a disused gunpowder workshop (la Cartoucherie) in Vincennes. Several of Cixous's plays were performed there. Daniel Mesguich is one of France's leading avant-garde stage directors (as well as being an actor, critic, and opera director); he staged Cixous's play *L'Histoire (qu'on ne connaîtra jamais)*.—Trans.

126. *L'Exil de James Joyce ou l'art du remplacement*, p. 38 [*The Exile of James Joyce*, p. 21; p. 14 for the second extract]. The pun "Allmen" appears in *Finnegans Wake* (London: Faber, 1975), p. 419.—Trans.

127. A later book on Hélène Cixous, the transcription of an inaugural conference lecture at the Bibliothèque Nationale to coincide with Cix-

ous's novel *Rêve je te dis* (Paris: Galilée, 2003), was to be called *Genèses, généalogies, genres et le génie.*—Trans.

128. Here we have departed from the wording in the King James Authorized Version, "a still small voice," not suggestive enough of Derrida's French translation, "*voix de brise légère.*"—Trans.

129. A thought here about a great thinker of speed who knew also how to recognize the very essence of life in it. Essentially life will have passed too quickly, it will have been so short. Nietzsche: "Against the value of that which remains eternally the same, the value of the briefest and most transient, the seductive flash of gold [*scintillement*] on the belly of the serpent *vita*" (*The Will to Power*, no. 577 [trans. Walter Kaufmann and R. J. Hollingdale, ed. Walter Kaufmann (New York: Vintage, 1968)]).

130. *Le Prénom de Dieu*, p. 157.

131. *Le Prénom de Dieu*, pp. 46, 49.

132. *Le Prénom de Dieu*, pp. 55–56.

133. *Le Prénom de Dieu*, p. 57.

134. *OR, les lettres de mon père*, p. 27.

135. That is, nostalgia + Algeria. The term *nostalgérie* had been introduced in *Monolinguisme de l'autre, ou la prothèse d'origine* (Paris: Galilée, 1996), p. 86; *Monolinguism of the Other; Or, The Prosthesis of Origin*, trans. Patrick Mensah (Stanford, CA: Stanford University Press, 1998), p. 52.—Trans.

136. Cf. "My Algeriance, in Other Words: To Depart not to Arrive from Algeria," trans. Eric Prenowitz, in Hélène Cixous, *Stigmata: Escaping Texts* (London: Routledge, 1998), pp. 153–72 (orig. in *TriQuarterly* 100 (Fall 1997): 259–79).—Trans.

137. Hélène Cixous and Mireille Calle-Gruber, "Entre Tiens," *Photos de racines* (Paris: Des Femmes, 1994), pp. 90–91; "Inter Views," *Rootprints: Memory and Life Writing*, trans. Eric Prenowitz (London: Routledge, 1997), pp. 80–81.

138. *L'Ange au secret* (Paris: Des Femmes, 1991) can also be read as a poem of atonement, between the ribs and the sides ("The house is not big. One has to slip between its ribs," p. 14. "To die facing birth's side, I came for that. To be thrown out right in the middle of a book," p. 15. "Once I was among those I despise and who are on the other side of the earth, I thought. . . . And nobody ever to ask for forgiveness," pp. 105–106).

139. *Illa* (Paris: Des Femmes, 1980), p. 139.

140. *Illa*, p. 143.

141. *Messie*, pp. 109–10. Further down: "I recognize its **mighty power** [that of the question]."

142. In this passage Derrida playfully combines the ambivalence of *nous nous* (each other, ourselves) with the feminization of himself as Cixous's alter ego.—Trans.

143. *Le Prénom de Dieu*, p. 205. In this first book, one could explore infinitely what I dare not call the premises or the matrix of the work to come. For example, on the side of the "living of life" and of all its signifiers, of the "consumptive" ("I envied the consumptive . . . Oh, to see my soul live toward my friend! . . . did not want to be deprived of the most intense, the most *empty* moment perhaps . . . " [p. 193, her italics—JD]), on the side of sides ("Although my friend was not by my side [*à mes côtés*] . . . " [p. 201]), on the side of the emptiness and of life ("nakedness of my life . . . of what is full and what is empty, seeing that every life is nothing but what I bring alive into the world . . . our life, the life on which my friend pursued his work. . . . It was death that should wait outside, in the unliving world of ghosts. Inside I carried on" [p. 202]), and on the side of the "knowledge that you know" ("'You know' 'I know' . . . I know that you know, I know even more, I know that I no longer need words. . . . Such is the peace that I drink to this knowledge that you know . . . the dream being what I had wanted to know, and I knew . . . " [pp. 204–205]).

144. The first half is a silent borrowing from *OR, les lettres de mon père*, p. 159.—Trans.

145. *Non pas pour changer de tallith comme de chemise, une chemise d'homme*. Here Derrida weaves a delicious sartorial metaphor on the French idiom *changer d'avis comme de chemise*: to be as changeable as the weather (literally: to change one's mind as one changes one's shirt).—Trans.

146. *Le Prénom de Dieu*, pp. 175, 176, 177.

147. *Le Prénom de Dieu*, pp. 181, 183.

148. *Le Prénom de Dieu*, p. 183.

149. The title of Cixous's novel can be heard as *il* (third-person singular masculine pronoun) and *la* (feminine definite article), but perhaps also as *il l'a* (he has it).—Trans.

MERIDIAN

Crossing Aesthetics